MindShifting

Stop Your Brain from Sabotaging Your Happiness and Success

VOLUME 1

BY
MITCH WEISBURGH

MindShifting
Stop Your Brain from Sabotaging Your Happiness and Success
Volume 1
by Mitch Weisburgh

Copyright © 2025 Mitch Weisburgh
Published by SkillBites LLC
www.skillbites.net
All rights reserved.

No part of this book may be reproduced or transmitted in any form or by any means whatsoever without written permission from the author, except in the case of brief quotations embodied in critical articles and reviews.

DISCLAIMER AND/OR LEGAL NOTICES

While the publisher and author have used their best efforts in preparing this book, they make no representations or warranties with respect to the accuracy or completeness of the contents of this book. The advice and strategies contained herein may not be suitable for your situation. You should consult a professional where appropriate. Neither the publisher nor the author shall be liable for any loss of profit or any other commercial damages, including but not limited to special, incidental, consequential, or other damages. The purchaser or reader of this publication assumes responsibility for the use of these materials and information. Adherence to all applicable laws and regulations, both advertising and all other aspects of doing business in the United States or any other jurisdiction, is the sole responsibility of the purchaser or reader.

Internet addresses given in this book were accurate at the time it went to press.

Printed in the United States of America

For more information or to place bulk orders, contact the author or the publisher at info@skillbites.net

ISBN: 978-1-952281-82-2 eBook
ISBN: 978-1-952281-81-5 paperback

Table of Contents

Preface vii

Introduction 1

Chapter 1: A Smarter Way to React 5

Chapter 2: Breaking Free from Our Scripts 23

Chapter 3: Silencing Our Inner Critic 53

Chapter 4: Mastering Our Mind 83

Chapter 5: Unleashing Our Own Brilliance 113

Chapter 6: The Realist's Guide to Happiness 143

The End? 159

Acknowledgments 161

Author's Resources 163

Dedication

This book is dedicated to all the educators who are preparing the next generation to live worthwhile and happy lives. You matter and we recognize your contribution.

Preface

Do you know anyone who often feels frustrated? Stressed? Angry? Resentful? Welcome to modern society. We all feel that way too often.

We would all be happier and more productive if we learned techniques to reprogram our own brains, to be able at will to change from an uncomfortable limiting mindset to one that is enjoyable, resourceful, and resilient. That's why we all need to learn to MindShift.

As I've learned more about how the brain works, and how we can redirect our feelings and thoughts, the idea that everyone should learn how to MindShift has become clearer and clearer to me.

And yet, as a society, how do we learn how to do that? There just hasn't been a straightforward easy way.

I don't understand why, but I decided to do something about that by first developing MindShifting courses and now this book.

My wife suggested that my preface be on my history of often being a little ahead of my time.

As she said, "You always come up with ideas and most people don't listen, but then a few years later, those ideas become mainstream. MindShifting is one of those great ideas. No one has heard of MindShifting, but what you are teaching is going to be mainstream sometime in the next ten years."

The path to creating and sharing MindShifting has not been a straight line. Before studying mindsets and figuring out the best ways to rewire thought patterns to produce positive, effective, and efficient decision-making, I was discovering new ways to streamline other aspects of my life to elicit positive, more efficient results. I'll start with business school, even though I've been an iconoclast since at least kindergarten.

I went to what was then called the Columbia Masters Degree Program for Executives in 1980–81. It was before the Executive MBA became so popular. We all worked at our jobs from Monday through Thursday, and then on Fridays we would attend classes with about 20 hours of homework a week. This was before Excel, Word, or Windows—everything was done using paper, pen, or typewriter on paper. After the first term I bought an Apple II Plus computer with VisiCalc and WordStar, revolutionary precursors to the electronic spreadsheet and word processing programs we use today, so I could be more efficient.

A month later I was on a train with my dad riding into NYC, and I was telling him that it was taking my classmates about 20 hours a week to complete their homework, but that with the Apple II it was taking me about five hours *and* I was doing a better job.

As I finished giving a few examples to my dad, this man jumped out of his seat and said that he'd just purchased an Apple II because he wanted to do cash flow analyses, but that the computer had to be assembled and came in five different boxes, and there were six different manuals; would I come to his office and show him how to do it? It took a couple hours for me to assemble the computer and then teach him enough VisiCalc to be effective, and by the time I got back to my office, I had a phone call from a friend of his asking if I could show him how to write documents on his Apple II. And then another call the next day. And then two to four calls a week.

Six months later, in January 1981, despite being told by Apple computer, the people who created VisiCalc, and the three largest personal computer resellers in New York City that there was no need to train people, I had started Personal Computer Learning Centers (PCLC) to train businesspeople on how to get their work done efficiently using PCs.

Up until PCLC, the standard way to teach people how to use a computer was to lecture about the history and different parts of the computer and then introduce computer programming.

PCLC introduced experiential hands-on learning to computer instruction. Class participants were confronted with business problems, and then they learned how to use the computer and software by solving those progressively more difficult problems, each one building on what they had learned previously.

PCLC defied conventional wisdom in at least three different ways:

1. That computers could make people more effective at their jobs
2. That people needed training in order to master the use of technology
3. That people learned best by solving problems

Our peak year was in 1995 when we had 7 offices, about 130 employees, and revenues of just over $10 million. During the course of PCLC's 18 years, I developed over 40 courses myself and trained dozens of people to teach, to develop courses, and to train other trainers and developers. As a group, we developed well over 300 courses. Now everyone uses computers, word processors, and electronic spreadsheets. Most of us probably couldn't imagine working without them.

In 2000, after I had closed PCLC, I was exploring how to start a business around online learning. I ran into a very distant relative who said he was building a company to prepare kids for the SAT exam online. He had hired some college students who were using a text editor and hard-coding HTML to create web pages that contained sample SAT questions and answers. Kids who wanted to learn how to get good SAT scores would go to the web page, view a problem, and then click a button to see the correct answer and an explanation. Then they would move on to the next problem.

It only took a few minutes for me to disagree with his approach and to suggest an alternative.

What I thought was needed was a novel system that could manage the content and the learning process to prepare for tests. Whatever content he wanted, whether to prepare for the SAT or any other test, could be added into the system, which could also inform the students and other interested parties, such as parents, how they were doing.

I designed and built a learning management system that was especially aimed for test prep. I was thinking of test prep as starting with learning objectives (these were the skills needed). Linked to the objectives were questions based on each goal, and also linked to the objectives was learning content in multiple media (text, graphics, animation, voice) that would explain the concepts and how to approach problems.

This type of individualized, learning-goal-oriented online learning is pretty commonplace today, but learning management systems were relatively new back in 2000, and the ones that existed were mostly to make the teacher's job easier, not the learner's.

Once the system was operating, we showed it to venture capitalists to raise money, and one of them, her name was Farimah Schuerman, suggested that what I should do was approach textbook companies and offer to help them digitalize their content.

As I started talking to textbook companies, it became apparent, at least to me, that to the extent they were considering online learning, they were looking to put the printed textbook online: basically a PDF, possibly with multiple-choice questions, and maybe with some video of a person reading the textbook.

I felt that online learning was a unique opportunity to make the content more interactive and engaging than a book.

Luckily I found some companies who agreed.

This was the launch of Academic Business Advisors (ABA). Farimah was my partner for 10 years, and ABA advised education publishers for over 15 years, me primarily focusing on systems and instructional design, Farimah on sales and marketing, and we met at strategy.

One of our hallmarks was that we rarely agreed. We would listen to a client talk about their plans, and both Farimah and I knew exactly what they should do, and we virtually always started out diametrically opposed. Our strength was that we were able to conflict constructively. We would hash out our differences, explore our different assumptions, and over the course of a day or so devise strategies that were substantially better than what either of us, or the client, could have come up with on their own.

The values of diverse viewpoints and the skills of constructively working through radical disagreements have traveled well to MindShifting.

The ABA business strategy was based on marrying product design with marketing and then iterating a strategy toward success. These are now hallmarks of Agile and Lean strategies that many organizations and consulting companies use today.

As a longtime advisor to education technology ventures, once a year I was asked to guest lecture at a workshop for EdTech entrepreneurs that was a joint project of Wharton Business School and the UPenn Graduate School of Education. In June 2017, UPenn sent out an email that the African Development University in Niamey, Niger, wanted US-based EdTech entrepreneurs to talk to their undergraduates about education technology.

My reply said that having an American talk about education technology to undergraduates in a completely different education system probably would not be worthwhile, but that I could conduct a session on Sensemaking: how the human brain makes sense of situations, how it uses those internal models to solve problems, how that process often leads us all down false paths, and that through understanding how the brain operates we could all become better problem solvers and also happier and more fulfilled.

That email ended up as an agreement to conduct 2 two-day workshops on Sensemaking for university students in Niger in February 2018.

That's when panic set in.

I had attended classes in Neuro-Linguistic Programming. I had read books on learning, managing, and making decisions. I had taught adults for over 30 years. I had even completed the six-month Landmark Education curriculum on living a life you loved. But I'd never taught Sensemaking.

I had six months, so I read about 11 books in fields such as economics, neuroscience, decision-making, military strategy, cognitive science, psychology, motivation, pedagogy, persuasion, management, and systems theory and put together what I hoped would be two days that would change the way these young adults would think about themselves, approach problems, make decisions, and work with others.

Then I flew to Niger and taught 2 two-day workshops to about 65 students between the ages of 19 and 26 in each class.

At the end of each two-day workshop, the participants all jumped up and cheered. These were techniques that they'd never been taught but that would allow them to think better, solve problems more effectively, and collaborate better. They were energized. That's how I knew that this material, which I now call MindShifting instead of Sensemaking, was valuable.

From that course, I decided that if the next generation could learn to

1. recognize when they were being misled by their own brains,
2. really solve problems instead of locking themselves into half-baked measures,
3. feed ideas off each other rather than lock horns over different perceptions, and
4. use results as feedback rather than as signs that they failed and gave up

that they would be more successful, happier, and able to work through so many of the issues we are leaving them.

And that's why I've continually developed and refined MindShifting over the last seven or eight years. I've focused the classes for educators, who would then use the material as they taught and also teach those same concepts and techniques to their students.

Today, there are three courses developed, and there are well over 750 people who have been through one or more of the courses. I know that the courses make a difference, because I see the reflections and feedback from participants. These are some of the ways MindShifting has benefited them:

- In their own lives, using MindShifting to overcome stressors and obstacles so that they are both happier and more effective in and out of work;
- For teachers, learning techniques to actively co-regulate students and ultimately teach them to self-regulate so that they can learn more, achieve more, and be happier;
- For communities and organizations, creating cultures of learning, curiosity, engagement, and collaboration so that people can work together as a community to meet communal needs; and
- As a bonus, for society, using our higher-level cognitive abilities to explore, collaborate, and listen to each other to work together to solve problems instead of the frustration and divisiveness we are all experiencing.

Each person who learns to tap into their resilient brain counts. But there are almost eight billion people on the planet. How would teaching 30–50 educators at a time reach enough people to change the world?[1]

Plus, while a course can make a big difference, how would people who had learned the MindShifting materials continue to hone their craft? How could they share success stories? How could they help and support each other?

My goal is to reach five million people, for five million people to have the skills to reset their fight, flight, freeze reactions to perseverance, critical thinking, collaboration, and innovation.

I don't have the answers, but here is how I am working to bring these skills to more people.

This book, which could be the first of a series of books, was written for two reasons: (1) so that more people, and not only educators, can become aware of these techniques, and (2) to be a reference so that when situations occur, MindShifting

---

[1] How many people need to learn MindShifting techniques in order to change the world? Estimates range from 89,000 to 550 million. On the low side, Price's law is that the square root of the number of participants is responsible for 50 percent of the work, and applied to social change, that would put a critical mass at about 90,000. Laura London of the McKinsey Consulting firm in "How many people are really needed in a transformation?" proposes 7 percent based on studies of 200 organizations. This would mean about 550 million people. Greg Satell in "To Implement Change, You Don't Need to Convince Everyone at Once" in the *Harvard Business Review* notes that for changing social and political systems, Professor Erica Chenoweth analyzed 300 incidents of social change and noted it takes about 3.5 percent of the population, which would be about 275 million people. With nothing to go on but my gut feeling, I'd be happy if we could reach five million people. Imagine five million creative, collaborative people tackling the world's problems while living happy and healthy lives.

practitioners can refresh or improve their practice by going back to the book. My hope is that readers will be able to apply the techniques to their own lives or even help others learn how to MindShift and to continually develop their MindShifting skills.

I teach teachers how to use MindShifting in their lives and in their classes. The hope is that they leverage their knowledge and give the children in their classes a jump-start to becoming happy, highly functioning adults. There are three courses:

1. MindShifting: Mastering Your Resourceful Brain teaches how to utilize the resilience and resourcefulness of your own mind even when your first instincts are counterproductive.
2. MindShifting: Flexible Mindsets for Long-Term Success teaches how to approach situations or problems in ways that maximize the chances of ultimate success.
3. MindShifting: Conflict and Collaboration teaches how to work with others so that conflicts become opportunities for improvement rather than destructive battles.

I have created two role-playing games: The Decision-Making Game and the AlfaCoop School Redesign Game. These collaborative problem-solving games simulate situations where players learn about and use MindShifting skills to overcome challenges in order to achieve individual and common goals.

I am creating an online MindShifting community for people who have already been exposed to MindShifting to learn and share MindShifting practices and techniques with like-minded fellow practitioners. This is a way for all of us to advance our MindShifting practices together and for everyone practicing MindShifting to know that there are other people who have their backs.

I am training trainers to train others in MindShifting. I can't reach everyone, so having a phalanx of skilled MindShifting trainers dramatically expands the reach of MindShifting coaching and training. Plus, other professionals will bring other perspectives and their own experiences into their teaching. We all learn from each other, and diverse perspectives benefit us all.

Can MindShifting reach five million people? As community builder and friend Laura Zug said, "Changing the world is not for the faint of heart."

As another good friend and renowned humanitarian Angela Maiers says, "You matter!"

Please help.

Introduction

Napoleon Hill remarked, "Whatever the mind can conceive and believe, it can achieve."

Jesse Jackson observed, "If my mind can conceive it, and my heart can believe it—then I can achieve it."

These quotes are both about mindsets. A **mindset** refers to the attitudes, beliefs, and ways of thinking that determine a person's behavior, outlook, and mental attitude toward a situation.

Everything starts with the mindset.

If you want to be motivated and persistent in overcoming obstacles, setbacks, and procrastination, those are mindsets. When you feel overwhelmed by obstacles, when setbacks make you want to quit or scream, when you can't seem to get started, those are mindsets as well.

Self-management, executive function, self-regulation, personal agency, and personal responsibility are mindsets.

Feeling stress, anger, anxiety, and demotivation are all mindsets, and so are feeling curious, playful, and confident.

Wouldn't you want to be able to switch from a mindset that is holding you back to one that allows you to be resilient, resourceful, innovative or perseverant? That's **MindShifting**. This book teaches you how to MindShift. We will cover over 50 different techniques you can use to shift from mindsets that hold you back to ones that propel you forward.

Here are some examples, from participants of MindShifting courses, of how people benefit from learning how to MindShift:[1]

1. My reaction to one of my cousins is always a reptilian one. I developed a repulsive attitude toward him and his actions. Even the mention of his name caused a very negative, repulsive attitude. I changed my reaction through MindShifting. Now, when I hear he is coming, I am able to take a breath, accept the situation rather than react to it, and move my thinking immediately into my prefrontal cortex by taking a quick moment to remind myself that (1) he is what he is, (2) I am able to find my stores of kindness and patience, (3) reacting negatively is never going to produce any positive results, (4) keeping a rotten attitude is hurting me more than anyone else, and (5) this isn't going to last forever. I have employed all three methods of the Self-Commander (chapter 4) to be able to sit and listen to his stories. It is a conscious effort to catch myself before I slide into my reptilian self and resort to emotional reactions.
2. Last Friday, my class returned from music really amped up because they got to use ukuleles for the first time. Everyone wanted to discuss it and tell how far they had gotten in creating their own song with the chords they had been learning. It made the transition to math very challenging. So, we spent about five minutes doing a MindShifting exercise. It really helped calm the class and reset them so we could transition back to math.
3. My husband was making a frittata and asked, "What kind of cheese sounds good?" I responded, "Swiss sounds good." A bit later I noticed he had shredded cheddar. I said, "I said, 'Swiss sounds good.'" "NO YOU DIDN'T," he yelled back. It was ugly. In the middle of yelling back and forth, my brain processed the best it could that this was a MindShifting opportunity. This gave me some strength to have empathy for myself and then to think about what was really important. What came back is to ask if I could share some of my thoughts and reflections with him about the event. I shared what I felt was really important, and he listened to me say that we do love each other, that I would love to be in a loving relationship with him, and I want to regain the hope of that possibility. We were able to kiss goodnight and say, "I love you." So it really wasn't just about the cheese.

---

[1] Every example used throughout the book took place. I have edited details of incidents for clarity, spelling, and grammar, and to hide the identity of individuals to protect their privacy. The names are all made up except for family members. My wife is my wife, my kids are my kids, and my mom and dad are my mom and dad. I'll just have to live with the consequences if I've included stories about them that they object to.

4. I decided to try to utilize focused action and empathy (chapter 6) when I went to see my parents for a visit. My father is very authoritative, pretty sexist, and very controlling. He is quick to anger and easily frustrated. Going into my visit, I was very calm and removed. This Jedi mind trick certainly worked, and it was so liberating and such a relief because my own anger and hurt didn't get in the way of our interactions. I was trying to help him with an online order and all the steps required. Despite all his cutting comments, we were able to solve the problem he was having with the order. I felt better to have helped, and I'm sure he was relieved too.

The human brain is the result of billions of years of evolution and may be the most complex system in the entire universe. The brain controls everything we do, and everything we do starts with the brain's mindset. In this book, you will learn how mindsets are formulated, how to recognize when a mindset may be holding you back, and how to switch to a more beneficial mindset.

You will learn how to walk into situations prepared with a mindset predisposed toward success. When life throws unpleasant surprises at your plans, when people oppose you, when your brain starts sabotaging your actions or your emotions, you will be able to recover faster. When you see others held back by their own mindsets, you will have tools to help them reset and tap into their own resourcefulness.

Armed with this knowledge, you will be happier and more productive. You will find that situations that used to result in fight or flight reactions instead become opportunities for innovation and collaboration—just like the four people above and the hundreds of people who have taken MindShifting classes over the last five years.

For seven years I've been curating ideas from cognitive science, coaching, economics, military strategy, teaching, business strategy, neuroscience, decision-making, sales, education, interpersonal communications, and complexity theory to understand how mindsets are formed and how to switch to beneficial ones. Each of these fields seems to have a slice of the answer. This book is an attempt to integrate concepts and methods from all these different disciplines into a coherent system with guidelines that anyone can follow.

I'm anticipating that some of you will read this book, gain a better understanding of yourself, and acquire techniques to live a better life. Others may find it more beneficial to read this book with friends or peers and discuss and adapt the concepts and techniques based on those discussions. Others may have particular issues and look up suggestions on handling those types of reactions. Maybe you will decide to use this book to prepare other people to be more effective. I'd love to hear your suggestions, your successes, and your questions.

Imagine if five million more people on the planet suddenly became adept at critical thinking, listening, creativity, collaboration, empathy, and perseverance.

That's my goal. That's why I wrote this book.

For readers interested in taking a MindShifting course, joining a MindShifting community, or receiving a MindShifting newsletter, visit these links:

- For the MindShifting courses, go to https://events.humanitix.com/host/mitchell-weisburgh
- For the MindShifting community, go to https://mindshiftingeducators.org/
- For the MindShifting newsletter, go to https://blog.mindshiftingeducators.org/posts

CHAPTER 1

A Smarter Way to React

Yesterday I was making a left turn from our side street onto a much larger road. As I pulled out, a new pickup truck, which was traveling at double the speed limit in the same lane I was pulling into, came around the blind curve, crossed the double solid yellow line into the oncoming lane of traffic without slowing down, passed me on the left, blared the horn, and then veered back into my lane just a few feet in front of my car. As it passed, I gave the driver the finger.

Why did I do that?

It was a quick reaction. The truck was speeding. It could have easily slowed down and stayed behind me. The driver was driving recklessly, unsafely. The driver was obnoxious. I was angry.

My adult son sitting next to me said, "Dad, did you just give that driver the finger?"

"Yes," I replied. "He was being a complete jerk and was driving recklessly. Maybe by showing my disapproval, the driver will be more careful next time."

Some of you might read this and identify with what I did. I had every reason to get angry. The other driver was obnoxious; it made sense to get that out of my system and give that driver a piece of my mind.

Others can read this and wonder, How could Mitch do something so stupid? How could he be so immature? Doesn't he realize that insulting that other driver could have prompted a dangerous escalation of the incident? And then, he had the nerve to defend his action?

I am siding with that second group. This was a rash reaction that doesn't reflect who I strive to be.

Luckily, my choice did not result in any harmful repercussions. But it does make one wonder. The human brain has evolved over millions and millions of years. I have studied the brain and decision-making and so should understand how to make good decisions. How is it that a reasonably intelligent human being could make such emotional quick decisions and then *defend* them?

Well, we all do that. We all hastily take actions.

Sometimes those quick reactions negatively affect our ability to achieve what we really want. We do it without being aware that we are doing it. Then we double down on why we are right.

The good news is that we can change, and we can help others change as well.

Let's start with learning about how we make decisions.

The model we are using will be a conceptual model of the brain that I first saw explained in the book *How History Gets Things Wrong: The Neuroscience of Our Addiction to Stories* by Alex Rosenberg. In this (oversimplified) model, the brain has three parts that are involved in decision-making and acting.

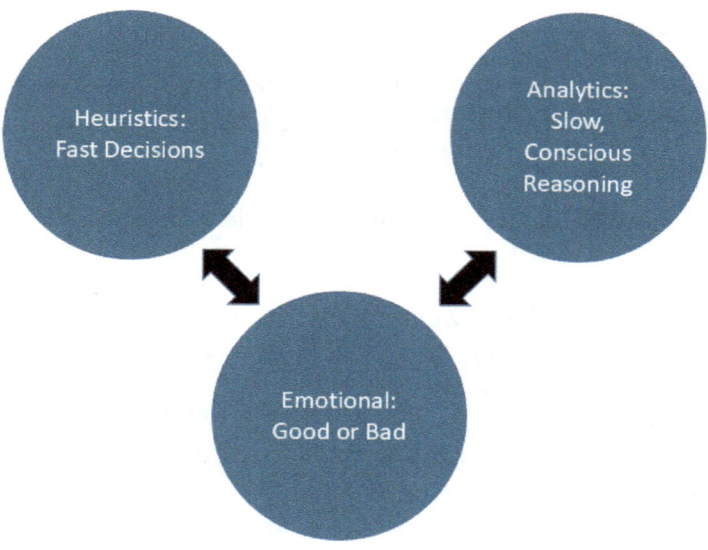

These are the heuristic (on the left), the emotional (shown on the bottom), and the analytical (on the right) functions of the brain.[1]

Heuristic means any approach to problem-solving using practical methods. When we refer to the heuristic function of the brain, we are including common sense, street smarts, mental shortcuts, rules of thumb, scripts, and habits—basically anything that doesn't require too much thought.

There are a lot of things that you can do without having to think about them. You don't consciously think about each step you take when you are walking; you can be thinking about something else or having a conversation. When there is a piece of food in front of you and you reach out and take a bite out of it, you don't have to consciously think about it. In fact, if we had to consciously think about each thing we did, we would be overwhelmed by all the mundane things we have to do every day. Being able to come up with possible actions subconsciously is a tremendous advantage that evolution has given us.

Heuristics allow us to function without having to stop and think.

The **emotional** parts divide things into good/bad. Good can be happiness, love, or calm. And bad can be pain, emotional distress, sadness, etc. The emotional parts of the brain judge things and decide whether we are in danger and also what we should do. There is no subtlety; it's just a binary switch: something is either good or it's bad.

The way the brain works is that decisions are *always* ultimately decided based on feelings and emotions. While all decisions are ultimately made by the emotional parts of the brain, that doesn't make the decisions wrong, and as we will learn, that doesn't make the initial decision a final one.

The heuristic and emotional parts of the brain work together. Together they are the fast-decision-making, unconscious parts of the brain.

Here's how it works. Through your senses you perceive some situation. Your emotional parts of the brain decide whether it's a good situation or a dangerous situation. Based on that assessment, your heuristic parts of the brain propose some action you can take without having to expend much cognitive effort—for example, run, walk, sit, eat, stop, yell, argue, laugh. The proposed action is passed to the emotional parts of the brain, which judge it: good, do that, or bad, don't do that.

---

[1] The brain is an incredibly complex organism. Saying that the brain has three parts and that those parts correspond to the limbic system and the prefrontal cortex is a useful simplification for the purposes of understanding how the brain makes sense of the world and how it chooses some action over another action or even inaction.

If bad, the heuristic parts propose something else, which then gets judged. Eventually, something gets judged as good, and that's what you do.

Functional MRIs have shown that it takes about 2/100–3/100 of a second for the heuristic and emotional parts of the brain to go into action. In a second, they can cycle through 20 or 30 potential actions, and most times a decision on what actions to take is reached in under a second.

And then there are the **analytical** parts of the brain, which are also your conscious parts, the thoughts that you are aware of. These are the parts that look over data, establish reasons, and may ask questions.

Studies show that it takes two to three seconds for the analytical parts of the brain to activate. That's a lot slower than the heuristic and emotional parts. Most of the time, by the time the analytical parts of the brain have woken up, the heuristic and emotional parts of the brain have already decided what to do.

For the vast majority of decisions, and this has been shown by neural biologists using fMRI and other means, the decisions are made, and *then* the analytical brain goes to work to justify the decision.

If I ask, Why did you go to a particular college, or Why did you accept your current job, you'll come up with an elaborate explanation using the analytical parts of your brain. But practically, it's because your heuristic brain came up with some actions, and your emotional brain said "good" to one of them, and only then did your analytical brain come up with some type of elaborate reason.

This sequence is the foundation of both *How History Gets Things Wrong* and Nassim Taleb's *Fooled by Randomness: The Hidden Role of Chance in Life and in the Markets*. Most human actions, most of your actions and most of my actions, are a result of some heuristic that was approved by our brain's emotional judge and then rationalized by our analytical part.

Why are the heuristic and emotional functions of the brain so fast, and why are the analytical functions 70 to 100 times slower?

A Smarter Way to React

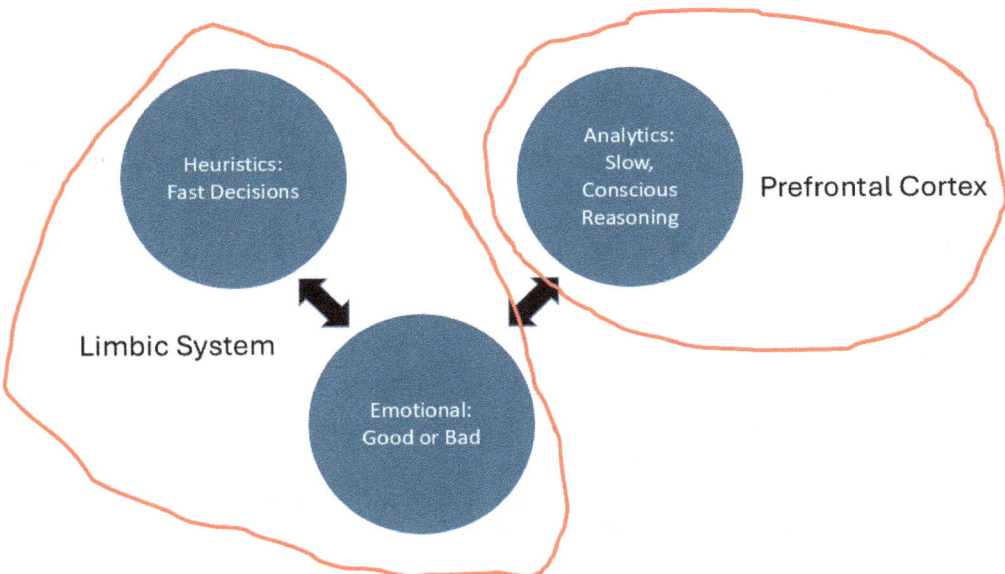

The parts of the brain that govern heuristics and emotions are within the area of the brain called the limbic system. The parts of the brain that are capable of reasoning and analyzing are in a different area of the brain, mostly in the prefrontal cortex.[2]

If you take your hand and bend the thumb in and then wrap your fingers around your thumb, your thumb would represent the limbic system and your fingers the cerebral cortex, which envelopes the limbic system; the prefrontal cortex is at the front of the cerebral cortex, right behind the forehead.

The limbic parts of the brain function more efficiently and faster than the prefrontal cortex. They function without conscious thought and are considered to have started evolving in animals long before the parts of the brain that are conscious and analytical.[3]

The number one thing the brain had to do was to keep the organism alive so that it could reproduce. All animals need food, and they need to react to dangerous situations. The emotional systems of the limbic brain are optimized for safety, to rapidly recognize

---

[2] More generally, brain scientists use three parts of the brain, not two. The brain stem is at the base of the brain. In simple terms, it is what connects to the spinal cord and runs most bodily activities. The cerebellum contains what we are calling the limbic, lower, or survival brain. It makes decisions and coordinates voluntary muscle movements, balance, emotions, and equilibrium. The cerebrum is the largest part of the human brain and contains the cerebral cortex. The prefrontal cortex is at the front of the cerebral cortex, just behind the forehead. There are actually over 100 structures within those three parts of the brain, and there are approximately 90 billion neurons, which is about the same as the number of stars in the Milky Way, and those neurons form over 100 trillion connections.

[3] Much of the information about how and why the brain developed comes from the book *I of the Vortex* by Rodolfo R. Llinás.

potentially dangerous situations and then focus all the organism's other systems on keeping safe. The heuristic parts of the brain were optimized to act quickly and efficiently in concert with the emotional system.

In humans, the types of actions the limbic brain decides upon before the prefrontal cortex even wakes up are:

1. Could this possibly be a danger?
2. If yes, then
   a. Should I fight, flee, or freeze?
   b. What are the actions I can quickly take that don't require any conscious thinking?
   c. What is everyone else doing?
   d. Focus the entire organism on that strategy by using fear hormones to shut out any distractions, including conscious functions of the prefrontal cortex.
3. If no, then
   a. What are the actions I can take that don't require any real thinking?
   b. What is everyone else doing?
   c. Is this a case where the prefrontal cortex could be helpful?

The prefrontal cortex is where **conscious** thinking and analysis mostly happen.

Here is a mapping of these different parts of the brain and their functions.

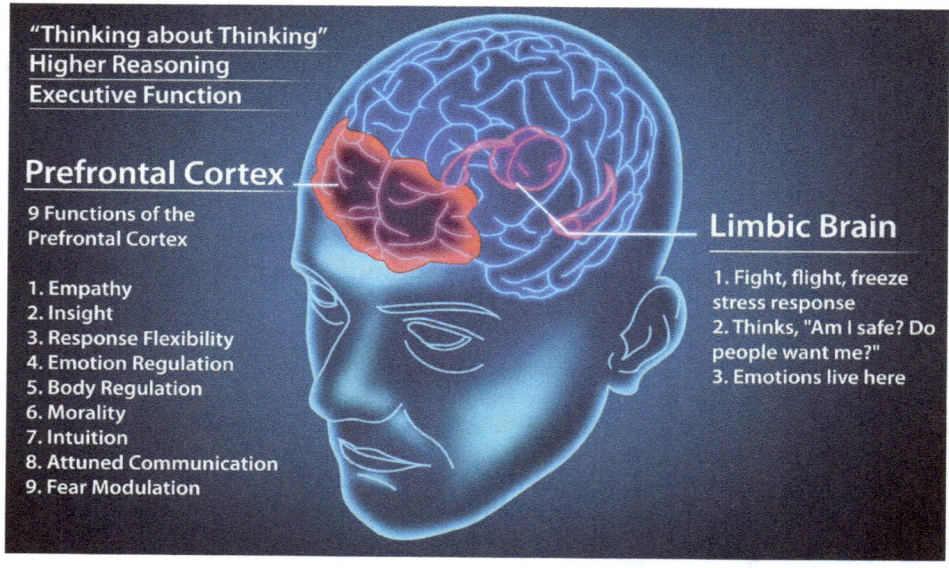

(Image from https://en.wikiversity.org/wiki/File:Blog_prefrontal_cortex.jpg.)

You can see the different functions of the prefrontal cortex. When we imagine what makes us human, it's mostly these traits: empathy, insight, creativity, critical thinking, morality, and communication.

These are all qualities that get shut down when we feel fear or anxiety.

These higher thinking and executive functions take two to three seconds after a stimulus to be activated. Before they even wake up, the limbic brain has determined if you are in any danger and often made a decision about what you should do.

Our prefrontal cortex is primarily, and by default, used to *justify* whichever strategy our limbic system has decided.

Karen was a participant in the course who saw this firsthand:

> Yesterday, I bought an expensive gadget. I was sure it was a well-reasoned decision. Its features were state-of-the-art. I needed a high-end device.
>
> Now, it just hit me. This was my limbic mind driving the decision, with my prefrontal cortex creating justifications for the purchase. Not only did I not need a new expensive device, but my existing one was working just fine. Reflecting on this, I see how emotions can subtly influence our choices, and I now know to be more mindful of my decision-making process.

As Jane McGonigal points out in her book *Imaginable: How to See the Future Coming and Feel Ready for Anything—Even Things that Seem Impossible Today*:

> We can overcome the natural, hardwired neurological response to adverse experiences. We can train our brains, instead, to detect the possibility of exerting control over outcomes in the future—by exposing ourselves to future scenarios and imagining how we might successfully react to them.

And that's the focus of this book, how to recognize when we are having a hardwired neurological response and then how to take control over outcomes.

As McGonigal says, "The brain assumes helplessness when exposed to adverse conditions. If we want to feel that we have any control over our own outcomes, we have to learn that we have power."

Of our heuristic responses, freeze is the first natural response that the brain learns. McGonigal goes on to say that after freeze, we generally learn flight and fight, then on to other heuristic responses.

How would we know, how could we recognize when we are in a freeze response?

Generally, when our limbic brains have chosen a freeze response, our prefrontal cortex will come up with a way to justify it, often with a statement like these:

- That's a long way off, I don't have to deal with it now.
- I am too tired, or I have too many other problems to deal with.
- That will never happen, or if it does, it won't be a big deal.
- I can't do anything about this, so why bother.

We have all used these and heard others use them.

When you give one of these excuses, or when you hear others using them, it's usually a sign of a limbic (or lower brain) decision, rationalized by the cognitive mind (or higher brain) that has been inhibited from creative or critical thinking by the hormones of fear and anxiety.

The responses that use the resourceful parts of our brain have to be learned. We have to learn that we don't have to just endure until the bad thing goes away, that we can tap into other people or that we can tap into our own resourcefulness.

We can easily recognize the freeze reaction in others.

We've all seen people who were sure they couldn't do something, yet as outsiders or interested parties we could see that it was all in their head. What generally happens when you try to convince them that it's really not that hard and they can do it?

In my experience, when a person says they can't do something, and I suggest, "Yes, you can," or even "Here is how you can," I generally meet resistance.

The decision "I can't" is virtually always a limbic one. The emotional parts of the brain have decided trying to do it is "bad," the prefrontal cortex has devised a reason why the person cannot do it, and that reason or rationalization, in that person's perception, is reality.

When you suggest maybe they can, the emotional parts of their brain evaluate your suggestion as a threat, even if the advice is well meaning. The result is freeze, or sometimes fight or flight. All resources of the brain get mobilized for that reaction, and none are left to critically evaluate whether, in fact, the suggestion is valid.

If we are really being honest with ourselves, it's not just other people who have that freeze reaction. We do that as well. We all have times when we are sure we can't do something, and when people try to convince us we can, we resist. The more forceful they are in trying to convince us, the more we resist.

Try this experiment.

Think of something you want to do or someone has asked you to do, but you can't do it. It can be something you are thinking of doing in the future, something you want to do now, or something you wanted to do from the past. It should be something you know you can't do.

Pause a moment while you imagine that situation.

Once you have something in mind, continue reading the next paragraph.

What are your thoughts or feelings as you think about this? Do you have that internal voice that's saying "I can't"?

For example, let's say that you want to teach an online course. When you start thinking about it, this voice in your head pops up: "You can't teach online," or "If you try to teach online, your course will never be good," or maybe "There are some people who teach well online, but you are not one of those people."

Perhaps you are thinking about retirement, and that voice pops up: "I will never be able to retire and live the way I want." Maybe it feels like a block, that you will never save enough or will always be in debt, or maybe you are very visual, and it just seems like there is a door that is closed and locked. If you are a feeling person, maybe you have an emotional reaction of disappointment.

This is what happens to most of us. We know we can't do something; we think about doing it or wanting to do it, and there is this voice in our head that just says, "I can't do that."

Now try something a little different.

Think of that thing you can't do one more time.

As you think of it, and you hear those thoughts or feelings in your head, I want you to say to yourself, "Perhaps I can." Just in that matter-of-fact, suggestive tone of voice. "Perhaps I can."

You're not saying "I am going to do this" or "I know how to do this." You're just opening up a possibility, maybe even a slight possibility. Think of this thing you might like to do. And when your brain says, "I can't do this," say to yourself, "Perhaps I can."

Did you do it? Did you think about doing it, hear the "I can't" voice and hear the "Perhaps I can" response?

What did you start thinking and feeling when you told yourself "Perhaps I can"?

For most of the people who have tried this technique, their brains started to devise ways that they could accomplish that task. Many talk about a feeling of lightness, like a weight has been lifted from them.

Maybe they needed to learn something. Maybe they could find someone to help. For the vast majority of people I know who tried this technique, their brains came up with a number of ways that they could get started so that they would accomplish that task.

In the case of teaching an online course, what might pop up are ways that you could make the course engaging, or material that you can offer that no one else can. It might shift away from a comparison that your course is not as good as other courses, or that it won't be good enough, to thoughts like "What could it be?" tapping into your creative powers instead of locking into your fears.

If you had envisioned a locked door, maybe the door opens just a crack. Maybe you still don't know how you are going to go through that door yet, but there is a perhaps. If you had this feeling of disappointment before, maybe there is a feeling of hope.

Here are some comments by people who have tried "perhaps I can":

- It changed my mindset and made me feel calmer.
- I noticed myself coming back to using that phrase around areas of my life that I hadn't realized I was telling myself "I can't."
- I love how I became more open, hopeful, and lighter. I can see how this works for my students and me.
- I notice a physical change when I say "Perhaps I can." The change is subtle but apparent. It feels like a shift and makes it easier to go forward with a stronger sense that I can do the task. Also, I've become more aware of when I slip into the "I can't" mindset.
- It made me feel like I could do something I previously thought I couldn't do.
- This is very similar to a technique I've used before. When I hear that voice saying "I can't," I respond with "I can't *yet*." This also opens up my mind to possibilities. I can't yet, but maybe I just need more practice, more time, or more knowledge.

If this happened to you just now, think about it. Your brain was always capable of creating those alternatives. But your brain was locked because you knew you couldn't. Your limbic system basically told your prefrontal cortex, "Don't think about this. Come up with reasons why you can't do it, but don't waste any energy or time considering ways you might be able to do it."

It might be that this "perhaps I can" technique did not have that effect on you.

One person had a phobia of driving on highways. When they tried saying to themselves "Perhaps I can," what came back was a thunderous "No you can't." That's a case where the new muscle of possibilities was not yet as strong as the experienced muscle of fear and anxiety. Perhaps one of the other techniques later on in the course would work for that person, or perhaps after using the "perhaps I can" technique on some less ingrained fears, it would become strong enough to overcome the phobia.

Some people try this "perhaps I can" technique, but there is no change. They are just as sure that they cannot do something as they were before they responded with "Perhaps I can." That's what makes us human. No technique in this course is going to work for every person every time. Perhaps this will work another time, perhaps it will work for another person if you try it with them, perhaps it will not work for you but some other technique will.

If "perhaps I can" didn't work for you this time, that's normal with any MindShifting technique. Sometimes an approach will work, sometimes it won't. It's like fixing a computer problem. You try the first thing; if that doesn't work, you try another. The better you get, the more computer problems you can solve. You'll never be able to solve every single computer problem, and you'll never be able to reprogram your mind for the optimal solution in every single case.

Sometimes obstacles are just insurmountable. A 70-year-old is not going to play basketball in the NBA.[4] A 37-year-old coming off knee surgery is not going to win a gold medal in tennis at the Olympics. Oh wait, never mind. Maybe they can if they know how to MindShift.[5]

The more MindShifting techniques you have, the more powerful you'll be. "Perhaps I can" is just one of about 50 approaches we will cover in this book.

If this technique worked for you, if you feel lighter about that issue and you started to perceive possibilities, then you just did your first MindShift in the book. You switched from a mindset of clarity that you could not do something to a mindset where there were possibilities.

In any case, whether it worked or not, remember this "perhaps I can" technique. It will be on the test.

---

[4] And so my hopes get dashed.

[5] In August 2024 Novak Djokovic became the oldest person to win the Olympic singles tournament since 1908 despite undergoing knee surgery in June of that year.

No it won't. There is no test. Living your life the way you want, that's the test.

When we say "I can't," even if it's subconsciously, the brain closes off access to its own creative and critical thinking abilities. And when we say "Perhaps I can," the brain can't help but to think of ways that perhaps we can.

In this case, you were the person who said to yourself, "Perhaps I can."

If you had said to yourself "I can" or "I know I can do this," you probably would not have opened up your mind. That voice would be more likely to push back because it already knew you couldn't.

Does this type of pushback sound like your internal dialog too?

> I'm going to lose 10 pounds.
>
> No, you know you can't keep a diet long enough to lose 10 pounds, and even if you did, you'd just put it right back on again anyhow.
>
> Yes, I can. I'll just eat less.
>
> No you can't. Look at that cookie. Just eat one cookie. Maybe you'll start that diet tomorrow, and one cookie isn't going to make a difference.

What if you wanted to open someone else up to the possibility that they could when they knew they couldn't? You are talking to someone who says they can't do something, and you say, "Perhaps you can."

We all are more likely to resist a suggestion that runs counter to what we know when that suggestion comes from someone else than if that suggestion comes from ourselves.

Only the person with the mindset can change their mindset. I can't change your mindset, and you can't change the mindset of another person. We can set the conditions to make it easier for them to MindShift, but we can't MindShift for them, and we can't force them to MindShift.

Sometimes we can say "Perhaps you can" to another person, and that will prompt their limbic minds to release their hold on the prefrontal cortex and open up to possibilities. It's even more likely to be effective if we can get them to ask the question to themselves. Perhaps we can try some conversation such as this:

> I believe you when you say that you can't do [*whatever it was*]. When you think about doing it, don't you have this voice that pops into your head that says, "I can't do this"?
>
> Now try something a little different.

Think of that thing you can't do one more time.

As you think of it, and you hear those thoughts or feelings in your head, I just want you to say to yourself, "Perhaps I can." Just in that matter-of-fact, suggestive tone of voice. "Perhaps I can."

You're not saying "I am going to do this" or "I know how to do this." You're just opening up a possibility, maybe even a slight possibility. Think of this thing you might like to do. And when your brain says, "I can't do this," say to yourself, "Perhaps I can."

What happened when you did that?

Does that conversation look familiar? It should. If you go back a few pages, you'll see it was just what the book suggested you do for yourself. And it tends to be very effective. Try it with someone. It's a great way to give someone access to their own creativity and resourcefulness.

Just with this little exercise, there is a lot to unpack about the mind. Let's spend some time on the relationship between attitude and perseverance, and then on the relationship between attitude and creativity or flexibility.

Consider the different states of confidence:

1. I can't
2. Perhaps I can
3. I think I can
4. I know I can
5. I'm definitely going to do this

As you read down the list of statements, you can imagine one's perseverance increasing.

Chart of Perseverance

Perseverance

The more definite you are, the more likely you are to get it done or persevere.

Why not go directly from "I can't" to "I'm definitely going to do this"? Why did we start with "perhaps I can"?

For almost anything, "I'm going to do this" or, even worse, "*You're* going to do this" is much more likely to trigger the limbic mind to resist and fight than to open up. The brain first needs to open up to the possibility, then a possible mechanism, and then finally it can commit.

From "I can't," start with "perhaps I can," then progress to "I think I can" or "I know I can" before trying to adopt an "I'm going to do this" mindset.

In addition to its effect on perseverance, the degree of confidence has a direct effect on creativity and flexibility.

We saw in the exercise that when we knew we could not do something, our creativity was blocked. Once we changed to "perhaps I can," the floodgates opened up.

What happens when we are positive we know how to do something or determined to do something in a certain way? When you are sure you can do something, how open are you to thinking about other ways of doing it? How open are others to alternative suggestions when they are sure that they know how to do something?

In other words, you are at your peak of being creative, or finding and evaluating different ways of doing something, when you are thinking "Perhaps I can" or "I think I can." And then once you start thinking "I know I can" or you commit, "I'm definitely going to do this," you actually are less resourceful—more persistent, but less resourceful.

"I can't" is a state of mind where a person is certain. The technique of "perhaps I can" opens up the mind so it is no longer certain and is willing to be flexible and creative.

When a person is certain, that person's mind is closed.

When we directly confront that closed mind, whether we confront our own minds or we confront others, we are likely to meet resistance.

Imagine a situation you know how to handle. When you are sure you know how to do something and you know exactly what you need to do, it's very possible that you are right; the action that you have chosen might be the best course of action for that situation.

It might also be that there are better courses of action. For example:

- A person has some money, and they decide to put all that money into one stock because a friend told them that the stock was sure to go up. However, all professional investing advice is that diversifying an investment portfolio reduces risk.
- A person hears from a coworker that they are earning more money performing the same job. They know exactly how to react, and they go to their boss and negotiate a raise, taking the first offer. However, researching the market value of the job first would give them a better idea of what to ask for and what they are worth.

Or it might even be that what you have chosen to do will make the situation worse. You will probably never know until it's too late.

- In a relationship, when a partner does something aggravating, the limbic decision to give an ultimatum could make the situation worse.
- A faucet is dripping, and the person is sure that they just have to turn the water off to the sink and tighten the connection, but what they end up doing is causing a flood, which then requires new flooring and bringing in a plumber to fix the bigger problem.[6]

---

[6] I know for a fact this can happen, because it did to me. And did my limbic system let me learn? Not that first time, because the second time, I also tried to fix it, with the same disastrous results. The third time? I called a plumber.

- You are trying to help someone with a computer problem and are patiently explaining where they should click, but they are so sure that they know what you are telling them that they aren't really listening before acting. They start randomly clicking around the screen, and they end up deleting files or locking themselves out of the system.

That's the way all of our minds work. When we are sure of something, we aren't open to other possibilities; we can't think creatively or critically.

Confirmation bias is the tendency of the brain to ignore any feedback or information that contradicts what it already knows to be true. Whether we challenge ourselves or someone challenges us, the limbic system assesses challenges as threats, and threats get handled by fight, flight, or freeze. Confirmation bias is human. We will talk more about cognitive biases in chapter 4.

Think about our limbic system's reactions in these situations where someone is certain.

Initial state of certainty	Directly approaching ourselves	Directly approaching others
I can't	Yes, I can	Yes, you can
This is what I am going to do	That's not the right way	No, this is what you should do
This person is wrong	No, I am wrong, they are right	They are right, you are wrong
I have to do it this way	I really don't	No, here is an alternative

Each of these responses, whether we are saying it to ourselves or we are saying it to another person, is most likely going to be met by resistance.

First of all, most of the time, and with most people, a person isn't even aware that they are certain. They just perceive a situation, and they know what they can or can't do. What they perceive is reality, and they are not thinking about their thinking.

Thinking about thinking is called **metacognition**. Most of the time, we don't think about whether we are sure or not. A situation occurs, and up pops an action served up by our heuristic parts of the limbic system. We know exactly what to do, and we just do it.

In the vast majority of cases, a direct approach of challenging that action is not going to result in any change, whether we try to use it on ourselves or on others. If

I'm thinking this is what I am going to do, and somehow my brain tries to challenge that with "That's not the right way," my emotional centers are going to regard that statement as a threat, and my prefrontal cortex is going to do its usual job of devising a justification about why it really is the right way, and then I'll double down on that initial action.

If a person were to say to me, "John is wrong," and I reply, "No, he's right, you're the one who is wrong," I'm more likely to trigger a fight reaction like "Here is why I'm right," "Here is why he is an idiot," "You always take his side," or something similar instead of "Thank you, I guess he's right and I'm wrong."

If we want someone's brain to be open, creative, or flexible, an *indirect* approach, one that doesn't make the person feel threatened, is much more likely to be successful. For example:

Initial state of certainty	Indirectly approaching ourselves	Indirectly approaching others
I can't	Perhaps I can	Perhaps you can
This is what I am going to do	Might there be other ways I could approach this?	And what other ways might you try?
This person is wrong	Maybe they are 90 percent wrong, but maybe I could learn something	Even if they are 90 percent wrong, what might they be seeing that you might be missing?
I have to do it this way	I wonder if I could come up with an alternative	If you had to find three alternative solutions, what might they be?

Metacognition is one of the most powerful skills we can learn. If we can recognize that we are certain about something, that we are sure, we can open up our own minds to other capabilities through questions or positive self-talk that doesn't directly trigger our fighting limbic mind. The examples in the table above may not be the exact ones that work for you, or they might. In practice, if you want to be creative and flexible, it first has to dawn on you that you are certain, probably because you are about to do something proposed by your limbic mind. That's metacognition, thinking about your thinking. Once you are aware, then you might be able to use a question like these to tap into your critically thinking, creative, and resourceful prefrontal cortex.

Again, it's most effective if a person can open *themselves* up to other possibilities. If we can say things like those in the second column to ourselves, we are more likely to open up flexibility, creativity, and critical thinking. These would be examples of self-regulating.

It's a lot easier to see that someone else is unknowingly trapped into a limbic way of thought or action. In those cases, it might be possible to take on a role of coach or co-regulator. A good co-regulator does not directly confront or challenge, because we've already seen that will more likely trigger fight, flight, or freeze. A good co-regulator will open up possibilities and perhaps use statements or questions similar to the indirect approaches in the third column above.

We can suggest, but it's even more effective if we can prompt a person to open themselves up with their own self-talk. We can help a person learn to self-regulate, when they learn to say things like the options in the second column to themselves.

Chapter 1 Review

What we've covered is a very simplified model of how the brain makes decisions. We sense some situation, and in fractions of a second our emotional parts of the limbic brain determine if there is any danger, if this is a threat. Our heuristic parts of our limbic brain come up with something that we could do, and our limbic judge decides yes or no. Together the heuristic and emotional centers decide on some action. Without even being conscious, we are generally certain that reaction is what we should do. If someone challenges our reaction, even if we challenge it ourselves, the emotional parts of our limbic brain regard that as a threat or danger, and they focus on a flight, flight, or freeze response and restrict our prefrontal cortex to merely justifying that action.

However, there are two ways out of that trap. Path one starts with metacognition, and we have just touched on one technique to tap into our resourceful prefrontal cortex with non-direct, non-challenging questions or statements, such as "Perhaps I can." Path two is that through training and learning, we can develop new fluencies, new heuristics, and thus improve our reactions.

If you are driving and an aggressive driver nearly hits you and cuts you off, perhaps your metacognition can act fast enough so that you don't do anything rash. Maybe on reflection you can develop and then internalize new and better reactions that will not escalate the situation. Understanding how to change our own or others' behavior might require understanding how scripts and stories affect our actions, and that's the topic for the next chapter.

CHAPTER 2

Breaking Free from Our Scripts

When my kids were preteens and teens, they would come home from school and our conversations would be like this:

Me: How was your day?
Kid: Okay.
Me: What did you do at school today?
Kid: Stuff.
Me: Did you learn anything new?
Kid: No.
Me: Well, what happened?
Kid: I'm going out now (or I'm going up to do my homework now).

What was going on in my mind at first was, "I'm a concerned parent. I love my kids. I want to find out how they are doing, if they need any help, and what they are interested in." And, as the conversation continued (abbreviated here), "They are being difficult. Why does this have to be so hard? Why can't they just talk to me like a human being instead of this angry kid they've become?"

You can probably figure out what was going on in their minds. "Why does he always meddle in what I'm doing? Why can't he just accept me the way I am? Why is he bothering me? If I told him anything, he'd probably just criticize me, so let me get away as quick as I can."

We were both locked into stories and scripts without even realizing it.

The story of stories and scripts is the focus of this chapter.

In the first chapter, we talked about a model of the brain where there are three parts that participate in decisions. The heuristic parts of the brain are all the things we know how to do without having to consciously think about them. The emotional parts of the brain work like a binary decision maker: "Yes, this is what I am going to do," or "No, this is not what I am going to do."

These two parts of the brain were formed very early in the development of animals. They were used to detect and react to danger and also nutrition. We avoid danger; we move toward nutrition. These parts of the brain activate in 2/100–3/100 of a second from stimulation, which can be from any of the five senses.

The parts of the brain that deal with feelings and emotions, and the autonomous actions we don't even think about, are part of the limbic system. People sometimes refer to this as our lizard brain, our primitive brain, our lower brain, or our survival brain. Animals could never have survived without these parts of the brain, and there is strong evidence that these parts of the brain developed before the prefrontal cortex did.

The ability to be conscious and think developed later in evolution. This is where many of our creative and critical thinking abilities reside. The prefrontal cortex is sometimes referred to as our higher brain, our Sage brain, or our analytical brain. And as we discussed, by default, our limbic or lizard brains often make a decision, then our analytical or prefrontal cortex merely provides a rationale for that decision.

Other animals have prefrontal cortices, but they developed more in mammals, even more in hominids, which include humans and the great apes, and even more in human beings themselves.

To a certain extent, it is the development of the prefrontal cortex that biologically makes mankind different and more adaptable than other animals.

The evolutionary advantage of having a limbic system that can rapidly respond, and a thinking system that is slower, is that it allows you and your brain to quickly focus on reacting to possible threats, and when there is no threat to be resourceful and adaptable.

Interaction of Limbic Systems and Prefrontal Cortex

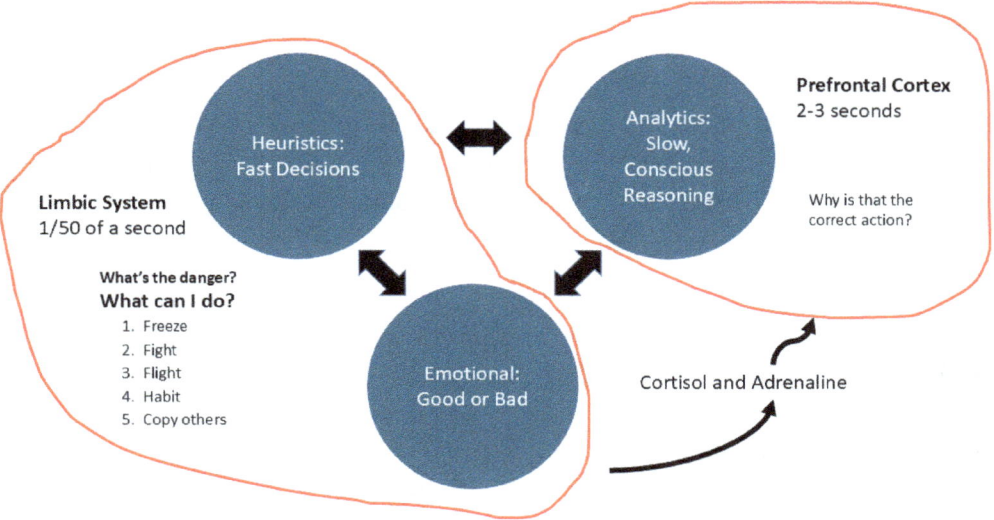

There are five types of actions that can be proposed by the limbic system. We discussed that the very first behavior adopted by infants is freeze, followed by fight and flight. When we learn a skill, behavior, or activity to the point of fluency, that behavior becomes part of our heuristic toolkit. Fluencies or habits are actions where we no longer need to consciously think about them as we perform them. Finally, our limbic systems have a strong propensity to copy or mimic what others are doing. We learn from others, and we also react to peer pressure and the desire to fit into groups. We even have a part of our brains, our mirror neurons, dedicated to copying what others are doing.

Those are the five different types of reactions of the limbic or survival brain: freeze, fight, flight, habit (or fluencies), and copying others.

Much of the time, we just react and aren't conscious of why we are doing something. We eat, we walk, we smile, we drive cars. If we do think about what we are doing, our prefrontal cortex will give us a reason why we are doing that. We stack eating because we are hungry, or because the food was there, or because there are people who are starving and we shouldn't waste food. But the prefrontal cortex really did not have a part to play in the decision; it is fulfilling its role to justify or rationalize our actions.

If our emotional parts of the brain, driven by the amygdala, sense danger or a threat of danger, they cause the release of stress hormones, cortisol and adrenaline. These hormones can heighten our muscular reactions to danger, allowing us to run faster or hit harder, for example. They also inhibit the functioning of our prefrontal cortex. The advantage is that we can focus on the specific action that was chosen: freezing, fighting, fleeing, some habit we are fluent in, or going along with the crowd. The disadvantage is that we are not able to explore, innovate, or think critically.

The amygdala is not capable of determining the severity of a threat. The possibility of making a mistake is a threat, the possibility of dying is a threat. To the amygdala, a threat is a threat. Threats trigger limbic emotional reactions, which then trigger limbic actions along with the suppression of any ability to think creatively or critically.

How many times have you been frustrated with someone because you can clearly see they are wrong, but they seem incapable of seeing it themselves? Perhaps a student, or someone who disagrees with us politically, and they are so sure of what they believe even though we can clearly see that they are wrong and that they aren't taking into account information that is right there in front of them.

Their limbic system shut down their prefrontal cortex. When that happens, they are incapable of taking in new information or reassessing. Only when their survival brain releases its hold will they be able to explore, innovate, or pivot.

It's a lot easier to see these biases and errors in others. The fact is, though, that these are parts of all of us. Our own family, our peers, people who disagree with us politically look at us and see us stuck in our beliefs, even though *they* can clearly see that we are wrong and that we are not taking into account information that is right there in front of us. We are generally not aware of our own biases, and if we were, we'd probably be horrified.

There are two opposing concepts at play, and they are both true. On the one side, so many of our actions and decisions are determined by our primitive parts of the brain. These can be detrimental to our short- and long-term well-being. But we will fight to defend them when challenged. On the other side, we are not locked into these suboptimal limbic reactions.

We are not locked in because there are two ways we can improve our responses:
1. We can train our heuristic parts of the brain with more skills.
2. We can calm our emotional limbic reaction and reset the brain to access creativity, critical thinking, and resourcefulness.

First of all, we can improve our skills and ability to react rapidly. When we learn a new skill and internalize it, we are building our heuristic capabilities. You have achieved fluency in many areas: reading, addition and subtraction, driving, walking, perhaps your work, and your sports. These are all skills that you had to consciously learn, then practice, and which eventually became second nature.

My wife and I take dancing lessons. When we started learning rumba, I had to learn the (male) foot movements to the basic step. Fast step with the left foot. Fast step with the right to bring the two feet together, slow step with the left foot forward. Forget about keeping up with the beat. I was lucky if I didn't fall or step on my wife's foot. By the end of the first year, I could do the basic steps of the rumba subconsciously, and I could listen to the music while I was dancing.

Driving a car, cooking, public speaking, learning a new language, and managing finances are all skills that many of us initially struggled with but that through practice we picked up fluency. They became embedded in our limbic brain, and we can now perform them with little cognitive effort.

Second, just because the default use of our analytical parts of the brain is to justify what we've already come up with through quick and dirty heuristics doesn't mean that we have to relegate it solely to that status. We can use our **higher order**, or what I sometimes call our **Sage**, parts of the brain to question our decisions. We can double-check the data or information; we can question if there are other possible explanations or paths.

What if we could recognize our own mental holes and, by ourselves, improve the way we think to look at other alternatives, align our actions better to our goals, or be open to data that might conflict with what we thought before? Wouldn't that increase our chances of ultimate success?

Self-awareness, or metacognition, is a key skill to self-improvement. As we learn to be better at self-awareness, we are more capable of learning and adapting, and as we teach students and others self-awareness skills, we help them on their journeys as well.

That's basically what you are doing when you say

- "Perhaps I can" or "I can't *yet*,"
- or "I've succeeded at hard things before, and I can do it again,"
- or "Maybe there is another way,"
- or some other constructive internal chatter that opens you up to new possibilities.

That's why the arrows go both ways in the diagram. By default, the heuristic actions that our emotional judge decides on get justified by our analytical prefrontal cortex. That's one direction, from limbic to PFC. We can learn to use our prefrontal cortex to challenge those and rewire or retrain our limbic system with new skills and actions and also change the way we evaluate what is good or bad. That's using the prefrontal cortex to alter our limbic decisions and capabilities.

Mark was a participant in a recent MindShifting class and noted:

> When I was coaching baseball, I knew that practicing the basic skills was the path to improvement. I had the same script almost every day of practice. It got to the point where the kids knew what to do next before I even said anything. I felt it was productive, but progress was slow. At some point I asked myself, "Could there be a better way?" I decided to come up with different routines for practice every day. Kids didn't know what was next. They improved at a faster rate and also had more fun.

Mark found he was locked into a way of being and doing. Just being aware of that prompted him to look for alternatives with a sense of curiosity. He tried varying his routine and found something that clicked, and the team took off.

Being self-aware means learning to recognize our biases, scripts, and stories, which are often hidden in our subconscious. When we question them, we often find better ways, just as Mark did.

When you tell yourself "I can't," that's the limbic system deciding that you can't, doing what it thinks is its job of protecting you from failure or danger. Then when you provide a reason why you can't, that's the prefrontal cortex providing a rationalization. Generally, that rationalization is in the form of a story or a meme. You don't even have to think: the situation occurs, up pops "I can't do this," and then, if you don't catch yourself, there is a story about why you can't, and that's it.

In Mark's case, the story was "practice makes perfect." Until he caught himself, that was it. Once he caught himself, he was able to modify the story and the routine: "Practice makes perfect, and variability makes practice more interesting and motivational."

A story is neither right nor wrong. Stories are simplifications that allow our brains to rapidly make sense of a situation and take action. Stories are convenient.

In many "I can't" cases, your limbic system and your prefrontal cortex are at first working together to build a story that sabotages your efforts to act. They are working as a **Saboteur**.

Often, when we directly challenge our story, or when someone else challenges it, our survival mind fights back.

Psychiatrist and author Phil Stutz, subject of the Netflix documentary *Stutz*, uses the term **Part X** for the phenomenon of our limbic brain inhibiting our ability to be effective. Part X is the judgmental part of you. It's an invisible force that wants to preserve the status quo, to keep you from growing or changing. It blocks your evolution and potential.

It does this by creating stories that we just take as being reality. Here is a great example.

I have a friend who is a grief counselor, and she and two counselors formed a three-person support group. Fast-forward a year, and she wasn't sure she was still getting a lot out of the group. She wasn't quitting the group, she just wasn't putting in the time, but she also wasn't telling them.

We can boil her potential actions down to three choices:

1. She could commit to being in the group, at least for a while, to see if it got better.
2. She could quit the group.
3. She could tell the group she felt she wasn't getting much out of it anymore and see what happened next.

Here is how her Part X was messing with her.

When she decided to stick with the group, her internal dialog was, "You just don't have the nerve to make a real change. This group isn't doing for you what you want, but instead of taking action, you are just taking the easy way out and not confronting people. It's just typical of why you will never succeed."

And when she decided to leave, her internal dialog was, "Oh that's just great, giving up again. You always start things and never follow through. These people are friends of yours, and they are counting on you, and you're just going to walk away from them and not support them. How can you expect people to like you when you are always letting them down? How will you ever amount to anything if you are always quitting?"

And when she decided to talk to the other two members and just give it a little more time, her internal dialog was, "Make a freaking decision already. Stop being such a wimp. Either do it or don't, but this is why you never get anything done, because you can't make a decision and take an action."

Brutal, right? Really, she had three choices—keep with the group, quit the group, or give it more time—and whichever choice she made, her own brain attacked her.

That's what happens with all of us. Whatever choice we make, our Part X attacks us.

This is how she defeated the Part X dialog. She spent about 15 minutes doing a meditation, and when the dialog was quiet, she made a conscious effort to listen to her heart and her gut. And they came back and told her that she should move on and find better uses of her time and let the group know that they had helped her in many ways and that now was a time for her to make a move to something else.

When she told them, they were relieved and told her they were feeling the same thing and thanked her for raising it. And when her Part X started attacking her for the decision, as it always does, she just laughed and felt centered.

Each of us has a Part X. Part X will always tell us we are not good enough, we are doing things wrong, we are too slow, we are too fast, we are victims, and so on.

Our own Part X or Saboteurs will always attack us. The first step is to be aware that when we are telling ourselves these stories, they are just stories. The second step is to quiet our emotional reaction to those stories. And the third step is to come up with a different story we can be comfortable with.

How to Win Against Part X
1. Be aware
2. Calm the emotional reaction
3. Change the story

What we *can't* do is argue with our Part X. We have to quiet it. At least for a while.

In the example of my friend, once she realized that her Part X was messing with her, she used steps 2 and 3 to overcome it. She did a mindfulness exercise to ground herself and then made a decision based on her values. When her Part X tried to mess with her a second time, she just called it out. When you say, "That's just my Part X, and I don't have to listen to it," you are calling out your Part X and diminishing its power.

Defeating her Saboteurs and then moving on with her life gave her great joy.

You can defeat Part X or your Saboteurs temporarily, but they're always going to keep coming back. On the other hand, Dr. Stutz maintains that the highest happiness of a human being is the process of actually defeating Part X or overcoming Saboteurs and creating something in the face of adversity.

If you think about the acts in your life that you are most proud of, you're probably remembering times when you defeated your own Saboteur mind.

Now that you are aware of your limbic mind, your Saboteurs, and your Part X, you may be better able to notice when they are aroused. Think back to situations where you felt paralyzed by internal criticism. When has that happened to you? Whatever you decided to do, your own brain told you how wrong and worthless you were. Those were stories; they felt like reality, but they were stories.

There are so many Part X stories that get lodged into our brains. Here is another one.

Sometimes, you're on a diet, and you see a dessert, and you start eating that dessert. What's the story? Maybe "I'll deal with the diet tomorrow" or some similar justification, right? "Maybe I'll deal with whatever this is tomorrow" is another story. How many of us have done that to ourselves?

That's Part X. That's our Saboteurs. Now you know about your Saboteurs. When you see a dessert, you know that your Saboteurs are going to start lying to you. They are going to start telling you that it's just one dessert, that you can go back to your diet tomorrow.

When your prefrontal cortex is in charge, or when you have conditioned your heuristic parts of the brain with effective reactions, you may be on a diet, and you see a dessert, and you pass it by. Doesn't that make you feel great?

Use these three steps:

1. Be aware. If you can tap into your metacognition, your self-awareness, perhaps you can realize what your Saboteurs are doing.
2. Calm the emotional reaction. Change where your attention is focused.
3. Change the story. How happy do you think you will be when you see that dessert and have the presence to realize that it's just Saboteur stories that are telling you that it's okay to eat it and then pass on that dessert?

That's changing the story. Instead of "I'll just eat that dessert," you've changed the story to "That's just my Saboteurs messing with me again. I really don't need that dessert, and I'll be better off not eating it."

Knowing it's Part X or that it's just a Saboteur telling you a story so that you will not do something makes it easier to do what you really want.

Stories are very powerful motivators. Let's dive deeper into how and why they work.

There are two different sequences of how the brain uses stories and actions. By default, these are the two ways our brains deal with situations.

How stories are used

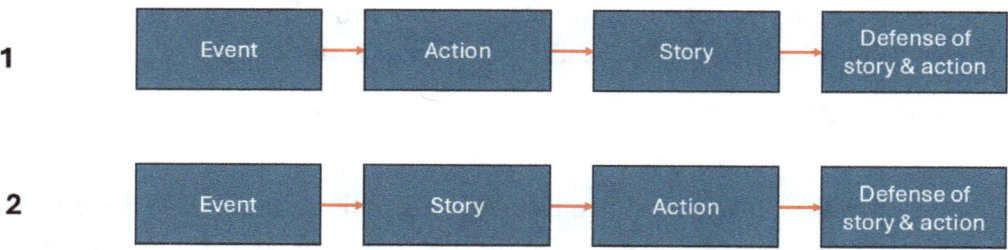

Expanding the decision-making brain model discussed in chapter 1, the first process is

1. We sense something has happened or is happening.
2. We process it emotionally to determine if it's a threat or not.
3. We cycle through actions we are fluent in until we emotionally approve of some action.
4. We act.
5. Our higher-order parts of the brain rationalize that decision as a story.
6. We process any results as justifying the story and action.

Once we build a story, the story determines how we approach the situation; our brains no longer need to construct a new one. Where we already have a story for a certain type of event,

1. We sense something has happened or is happening.
2. We find a story about that type of event and what to do.
3. Based on that story, our heuristic parts of the brain propose an action.
4. Our emotional parts of the brain accept that action (we cycle through fewer actions, because we already know what to do).

In either case, once we have an action and story, any thoughts or arguments against that action are processed as threats, which causes our limbic system to release fear hormones and trigger what is most likely a fight, flight, or freeze reaction while disabling our higher-order abilities to innovate, take in new information, or think critically.

Stories take on a life of their own, and we don't even think about them; we just follow them blindly. Sometimes that's helpful, and sometimes it's detrimental.

- "This child is difficult" is a story, and that affects how we interact with that child.

- "This child is wonderful but just made a mistake" is a story that would lead to very different interactions.
- "This teacher doesn't like me" is a story, and that affects how a student interacts with a teacher.
- "This teacher is trying to bring out the best in me" is a story that would spark different student-teacher interactions.

In schools, when a bell rings at the end of class, students and teachers have a story about what they are supposed to do, and they don't really have to think about it. When our boss comes in to observe or talk with us, we have a story about why and what is going to happen. As parents, when we talk to a teacher about our child, we have stories about how the teacher and child are interacting and a story about how the teacher will interact with us. As a teacher, when we talk to a parent about their child, we have stories about how the parent and child interact and how that parent will interact with us.

We have stories all the time, and most of the time we are not even conscious of them:

- I'm not a good speaker
- I am stupid
- I am fat
- I don't have time to do this
- No one can do this but me
- Pollution by selfish businesses is ruining the earth
- We can't do anything about reducing our dependence on fossil fuels because it will ruin the economy

Every one of those is a story. Some are clearly false. Some are shortcuts based on observed information. Some are harmful. Some may be helpful. They are all stories, simplifications that allow our brains to rapidly make sense of a situation and take action.

And with many stories, once the story pops into our heads, our actions become automatic. It's as if we are thoughtlessly following a script.

Stories are not the situation; each story is just a *possible* explanation that allows you to make sense of the situation. "I can't" is a story. Often, "I can't" is a story told to you by your Part X. It's like your limbic mind is writing a play and the rest of you is just following the script.

When you say "Perhaps I can," you are changing the story. You are opening up to the possibility that perhaps you can. Just saying "Perhaps I can" to yourself might be enough to (temporarily) defeat your Part X or Saboteurs. And "I think I can," "I know I can," "I know exactly what to do," and "I absolutely can and will" each represent a different story or perception. When you say "That's just a Saboteur, and I'm going to walk right past that dessert," you are changing the story. When you say, "I'm going to feel so good tomorrow that I passed by that dessert," you are moving off of the script. You are in control.

In the past we've all just accepted these stories. All people do. We say, "We can't," so we don't. We say, "I don't have to do this right now," so we don't and then get distracted and just don't do it. Similar to the maxim "whether you think you can or you can't, you're right," we construct what we call reality.

Social workers and psychologists call these actions scripts, like a script that actors read from in a play or movie, or you can also think of them as habits. They are programs that you follow without having to think. In the scripts we just talked about, you see something you'd like to do, you react with "I can't" or maybe "I'll deal with this tomorrow," and then you don't have to think about it anymore.

Here is a different story affecting perception.

One of my first jobs was as a salesperson, and one of my sales trainers told me this story. There was a shoe company that wanted to expand internationally, so they took two of their best salespeople and sent them to two different countries. The next day they heard from both people. One said, "In this country, no one wears shoes. This country is a waste of time, I'm coming back." The other one said, "In this country, no one wears shoes. Send over more shoes, we're going to make a killing."

The reality was that people were not wearing shoes. Whether that closed off opportunity or whether that opened up opportunity were just stories. But to the people telling those stories, the story was the reality.

Stop and think for a moment. If you are in a position where you can, read each of these questions, close your eyes, and think for a minute or two before opening your eyes and reading the next question.

- How did the stories these two salespeople told determine their actions?
- What are some examples of stories and scripts you have that determine your thoughts and actions?
- What are some examples of stories and scripts that seem to be determining the thoughts and actions of people you interact with?

We are all struggling to stay afloat in an ocean of stories and scripts.

Breaking Free from Our Scripts

Efficient Sensemaking

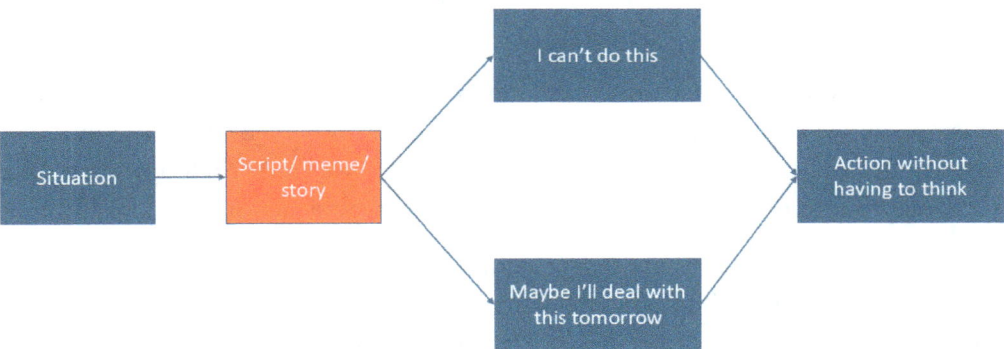

When we buy into a story or follow a script, we are acting without having to engage the parts of our brain that are creative or capable of critical thinking. In fact, those parts of the brain are inhibited.

When our stories are the result of our Saboteurs or Part X, the stories and our actions end up blocking us from our potential, they stop us from trying, or they result in us saying or doing things that are counterproductive to our goals.

Now that you're aware of Saboteurs and Part X, can't you see the connection between stories and actions, and also that we can create different stories?

It's easier to see how *others* are trapped by their stories and scripts, right? But as you practice, you'll start building this metacognitive skill of becoming aware of your own stories, and it will be a very powerful force in your life.

We Can Control the Story

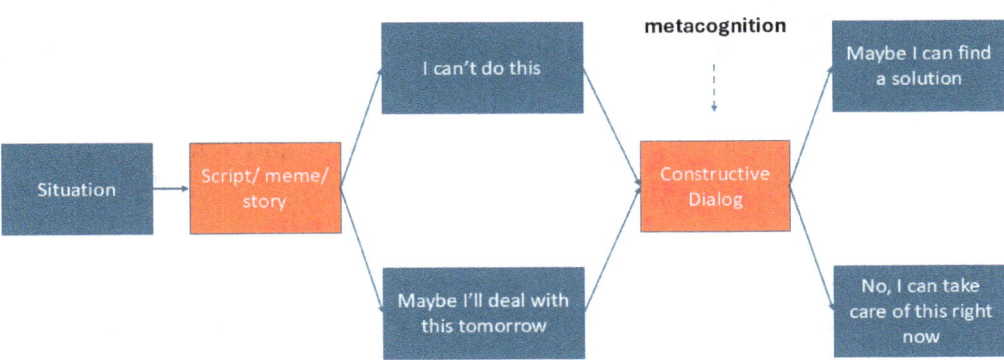

Very often our reactions are practically instantaneous. Somebody says something and we react, or we see something and we react.

All animals do this. An animal sees food and it eats. An animal sees a predator and it retreats.

People are animals. We react the same way; we use the same limbic reaction mechanisms. One of the things that makes people special is that we have a highly developed prefrontal cortex, and we can *change* the story; we can write our own scripts, thus adapting to changes in the environment and new situations.

When you react to situations using stories and scripts, you're using your limbic parts of your brain. When you use constructive dialog to question or change the story and script, you are engaging your prefrontal cortex.

This is reprogramming our own minds.

In many of the examples so far, we can clearly see that reprogramming our minds, overriding our limbic reactions, is advantageous.

But there must be advantages of stories and scripts, right? Otherwise, why did they evolve and survive?

Constructing meaning is work and takes time.

We construct meaning

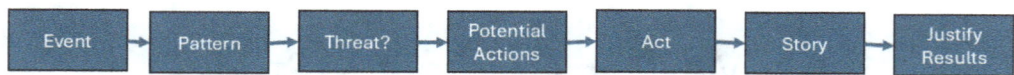

The human mind is a storytelling machine. Whatever we observe prompts us to formulate patterns, and we create stories. That's work. It takes effort to create a story the first time.

We look at something new—let's call it an event. The mind perceives a pattern: "Oh, this is like this" or "This happened, then this happened, so the first thing must have caused the second thing."

Then we construct a story: "When *x*, then *y*" or "Whenever *y*, then it's because of *x*." Consider these two story-building processes about public speaking for the first time.

Scenario 1:

1. Knowing you are about to get up and speak
2. Feeling the heart race and noticing sweat starting before speaking
3. Interpreting these as signs of impending failure
4. Experiencing anxiety and fear of embarrassment
5. Considering different options such as leaving, freezing, rushing through the speech, or taking deep breaths and relaxing
6. Rushing through the speech
7. Developing a story that you are no good at speaking and avoiding any other opportunities to speak publicly

Scenario 2:

1. Knowing you are about to get up and speak
2. Feeling the heart race and noticing sweat starting before speaking
3. Interpreting these as signs of impending failure
4. Experiencing anxiety and fear of embarrassment
5. Considering different options such as leaving, freezing, rushing through the speech, or taking deep breaths and relaxing
6. Taking a deep breath and relaxing, and then giving a speech to a standing ovation
7. Developing a story that while there is some stress in giving speeches, you are good at it, and you enjoy the results

Either one of these scenarios is work, and whether a person takes the first or second is to some extent a matter of luck. Once taken, the story and script take on lives of their own. The next time an opportunity to speak presents itself, our actions will be faster. Whichever story we told ourselves will determine our action.

We take some action, and there is some result. Our brains are designed to use those results to justify the story and action and to use them in future situations.

Imagine if we had to go through the meaning construction process with everything we did. Think about life without scripts.

It's a lot of work to finally arrive at something that works when you don't have any stories or scripts to guide you, right?

Imagine you're a new teacher. You are trying to teach, and you see Maria talking to a few other students. You see they are not paying attention, and observe a few more students joining in. You have to think about what to do, and while you're thinking, more students are starting to talk. You eventually raise your voice to Maria and discipline her, and the conversation stops. You can go back to teaching, but this has taken minutes out of your teaching time, and you really had to think hard to figure out what to do.

Our brains build a shortcut. Instead of constructing a story and action each time a similar event happens, they store a story and script, so that the next time we can react faster and with less effort. The event occurs, we select a story and action or script, and we act.

Now imagine that we go through that effort the first time or two we encounter a certain type of situation. If the result is something we can live with, and we internalize that story and action, then we never have to stop and think again; we can just go into script mode. "Maria is disrupting class. I need to discipline her." We don't have to evaluate, analyze, think, innovate, or reevaluate our teaching practices. It's relatively easy and fast. Student disrupts. Student gets disciplined. Student stops disrupting. That's the story.

We build shortcuts

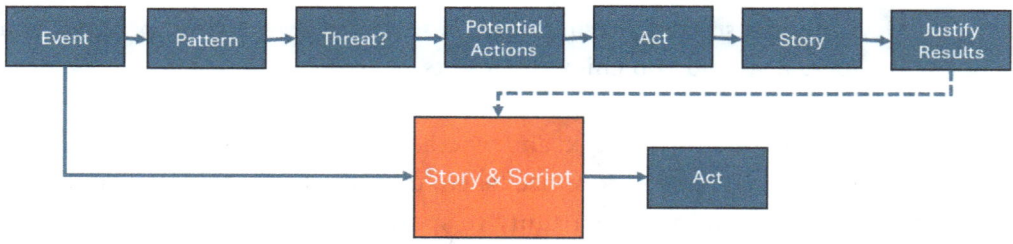

Successful stories and scripts become embedded into our heuristics.

We see a pattern and we react, so it becomes a script, habit, generality, or rule. We don't have to think; we just need to follow the rule or script and we'll be okay. The scripts become part of our heuristic mind, and we already know that this part of the mind activates in a few hundredths of a second, while our thinking minds take two to three seconds to go to work.

Every time a situation or event triggers a story or script, we just do it without having to think about it. Either the event triggers the story, which then triggers the script, or we react to the event using a script and when questioned access the story.

Creating a new idea may be fun, interesting, and beneficial. But it's work, and by default the brain looks to reduce work. We have evolved to be able to build scripts because they are fast and efficient.

Let's say you are driving. You see an octagonal red sign. What do you do? If you're my wife, who bicycles a LOT more than she drives, you slow down, decide if you can make it through without being hit, and continue along without stopping. If you're like me, when you get to the crossroads, you stop, look both ways, and once it's clear, you drive on. In both cases, there is a stimulus or event, then a heuristic limbic response. If someone asked you why you did what you did, you could give them the story, but in the moment, you probably didn't even think of it.

Imagine the time and effort, and possible errors and danger, that might result if we had to consciously construct a response. You see an octagonal red sign. As you get closer, you can read that it has the word "stop" in the center. Hopefully you are not traveling too fast, and you can slam on the brakes before you come to the crossroads. If not, hopefully no one is coming and hits you. Once you are stopped, what do you do? Do you wait for the stop sign to say "Go"? No, it's a painted sign; it's not going to change. How long should you wait until you can go? Maybe if the road is clear you can start up again. And so on.

Now imagine what happens when our heuristic reaction and story get challenged.

When someone questions or argues with our story, or when our results aren't what we desire, our limbic minds regard that as a threat. We disregard the feedback, and we filter the results so that they fit into our story.

I'm driving and stop at a crossroads. You might say to me, "We are in a hurry. You didn't need to take that long at the stop sign, no one was coming." My amygdala is going to wake up, and my internal dialog will be "You are being threatened, defend yourself." And I will likely attack back, "It's the law. The law is you stop for stop signs. Some of us are ethical and follow laws."

Or imagine me in the car while my wife is driving. What do you think happened the first time I questioned why she didn't stop at a stop sign? And what do you imagine my learned heuristic response is now, after 40 years of marriage, when she drives through a stop sign?[1]

As we get older, we develop and build up our inventory in these patterns. For example, we learn that a certain piece of data represents a cat, and this is how we can react. But another piece of data represents an angry person, and if we confront

---

[1] Yes, once or twice I did remark that my wife went through stop signs. Suffice it to say that I don't anymore.

one of these, we are in some type of danger, and our reactions need to be different.

The more scripts and stories we have, the less often we have to use our prefrontal cortex to explore, analyze, and innovate. Our brains fall into habits and fluencies, which is very efficient but which also can limit our prefrontal abilities.

The natural, effortless way to react to new situations is not having to think at all, when we can just use an existing pattern. And so the brain often looks at a situation, matches it to an existing story, and discards information that does not fit. Discarding information that does not fit our story is a type of cognitive bias that is hardwired into all our brains; confirmation bias is ignoring or just not seeing information that contradicts what we already know.

The next most effortless way is to find an existing pattern or story in our brains and make some minor adjustment. This is a foundation for good instruction: find out what the learner already knows and is interested in and build from there. Building on what learners already know makes it a lot easier for them to learn than treating each skill or piece of knowledge as something completely new.

I mentioned earlier that my wife and I take dance lessons. We are constantly learning new steps. When we see how a sequence of steps is built on something we already know, we can often master it in a couple of weeks. When we are introduced to a sequence that seems completely new, it can take months for us to be able to perform it fluently. Both our instructor and we make an effort to find similarities and advance from what we know rather than treat each new routine as something completely new.

Stories help us learn

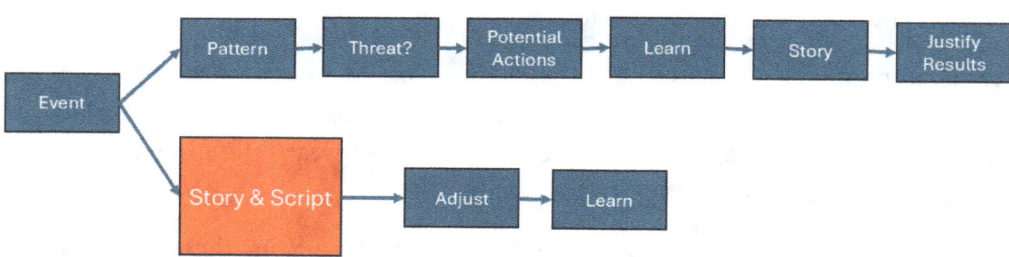

Our brains use stories and scripts to quicken the pace of learning. Usually when we learn, we base our learning on something we already know. Learning is work, and the easiest way to learn is to fit what is new into what we've already experienced. As we are learning, our brains try to make that process efficient by fitting new information into patterns we are already familiar with. When we teach others, we can make the learning process easier for them when we link what we are teaching to things that they already know. When students know how to count, we teach them how addition is built on counting. Then we build on their knowledge of addition to teach other math skills like subtraction or multiplication. When we encounter a problem, we try to find something similar that we have encountered in the past and adapt that solution or build from that solution to handle this new problem. When we learn how to drive, if we already know how to ride a bicycle, we can build on those skills to learn more quickly how to drive.

Because stories are simplifications, sometimes this leads to suboptimal limbic learning. If we know how to react to stop signs because we are bicyclists, then we might adopt unsafe practices toward stop signs when we learn to drive. Nothing is perfect.

While we are learning, our brains are working hard. When we operate from habits of fluencies, our brains are more efficient.

When you teach a child something brand new, it's a lot of work for you and also for the child. The child may struggle. The next time they encounter that situation, it may be easier, but they still might have to think about what they are doing. When you provide opportunities for that child to practice, they transfer that knowledge to their limbic brains and the parts of the nervous system that handle unconscious tasks, and the knowledge or skills become scripts. That's the purpose of practice.

Whenever we teach or coach or manage, to the extent we can help the learner attach that knowledge or skill to something they already know, we are making it easier for them to learn. If a child is interested in baseball, and if we can relate what they are learning to baseball, we can make it a lot easier for the student to learn. For example, if we are teaching fractions and decimals and the person is interested in baseball, perhaps we can relate them to batting averages or winning percentages.

Perhaps there is an employee who needs to learn to manage a project while also learning project management software. It's possible to have them learn the software step by step: what the software does, how it works, and what the features do. It's also possible to relate managing projects in business to other things the person has done, and as you go through the different functions of project management you can also show how they are done in the software. That approach is going to be more interesting and relevant, and the employee will most likely progress a lot faster.

You probably already intuited, or you learned, that providing an appropriate context makes learning easier. But now you have a better understanding of the biological basis of why that is true.

If the mind can go into autopilot, it uses far less energy, and if it can learn by relating new knowledge and skills to what it already knows, it will learn faster and with less effort. Our brains have evolved with two priorities. Priority number one is survival. Scripts and stories allow us to adapt quickly to danger and to learn quickly about new dangers. Freeze, fight, and flight are our first three survival skills. The second priority is to preserve energy. The brain is about 2 percent of a person's body weight, but it burns about 20 percent of a person's calories. The harder it works, the more calories required. Learning is work. Thinking is work. Creating stories is work.[2]

Scripts and stories allow us to be efficient. They save time and effort. When we build on them, we can learn faster. We can react faster. That is why they are part of our human toolkit.

While they have advantages, stories and scripts also prevent us from being creative and adaptable. Once we are in a story and script, unless we have the presence to realize what is happening and question it, we follow it blindly whether it is helping us or not in that situation.

We are also capable of building new stories and scripts, and often those new capabilities can enhance our heuristics. That's a prime function of learning and repetition, to learn something well enough so that it becomes part of our heuristics.

---

[2] Wouldn't it be great if that meant that we could lose weight just by thinking? I've spent a lot of time trying to find research that supports that, and it seems that every report or article upholds the same conclusion: cognitive activity does not lead to weight loss. However, I'm going to play my confirmation bias card here, and I'm going to ignore all those studies. I am going to stick to my story and go on believing that when I think, I am burning calories and losing weight. So far, every scale I've tried is broken, but eventually I'll find one that works and supports my belief.

The story that we believe influences the actions that we take, and the actions that we take influence the story that we believe. The story and script also influence what we perceive. The result is confirmation bias. The human brain is primed to accept information that confirms what it already believes, and it is also primed to discard information that contradicts what it already believes.

The human brain is also primed to detect patterns and connections, even when they do not exist. We then develop stories and act based on those patterns and connections. If a coin flip results in tails three times in a row, many people will predict that the next coin flip will also be a tail because they see a pattern and generate a story, such as "we are on a roll with tails." The term for this cognitive bias is **apophenia**, and it exists in other animals as well. One of the best books on apophenia is Nassim Nicholas Taleb's *Fooled by Randomness*, which describes both historical and present-day cases of decision-making influenced by false pattern recognition, and techniques we can use to double-check ourselves.

Taleb pointed out a B. F. Skinner experiment that demonstrated this bias applies to other animals as well. B. F. Skinner was an American psychologist in the 20th century, one of the pillars of behavioral psychology, and probably best known for his experiments on the effects of conditioning.

Skinner conducted a lot of experiments that showed how the use of rewards or punishments could influence behavior in people and many types of animals, especially mice and birds. For example, he'd put a bird in a box that had one or more buttons. And each time a bird pecked at one specific button, food would appear. And the birds would learn to peck at the button when they wanted food—they would establish that connection.

In one series of experiments with birds, he randomized the appearance of food. Food didn't appear after any particular action, just at some random time intervals. And guess what happened?

One bird might hop on one leg, and food would appear. Then the bird might turn its head, and nothing would happen. Then a few seconds later, it would jump on its foot then turn its head and food might appear again.

After a period of time, the birds developed elaborate rituals they would go through in order to trigger the appearance of food. One might turn its head counterclockwise and jump. Another would bang its head against a spot on the wall. But none of these actually had any effect on whether or when the food would appear. The food appeared at random intervals.

People also develop elaborate behaviors that they think are having an effect on events that are basically random.

Remember the movie *Bull Durham*, when the rising phenom pitcher happened to be wearing lady's hosiery on a day he pitched a shutout? For the rest of the movie, he wore lady's hosiery every time he started.

As outsiders, we can see that these behaviors in birds or in other people don't actually accomplish what they are meant to. When we look at older civilizations, we often call their beliefs, which were used to explain the world or predict the future, myths.

Apophenia surfaces in many of our everyday beliefs and actions:

1. Lucky numbers: people assume numbers have special meaning based on their personal experience, such as believing that their birth date is a good luck number to use in a lottery.
2. The hot hand: people believe that a winning streak (in sports, the stock market, or cards, for example) makes it more likely that the winning streak will continue.
3. Conspiracy theories: people connect seemingly unrelated events or loose connections to form a grand narrative that will, of course, be denied by those who are clinging to power.

4. Anecdotal data: people extrapolate from one or two instances, as in many health fads and diets where people make self-diagnoses, that sometimes result in inappropriate and harmful treatments.
5. Technology decisions: people are blinded by a new technology that will disrupt existing practices and invest time, money, and effort to achieve some goal that does not materialize.[3]

Remember the stories resulting from the example of giving a speech? With an "n" of 1, one person concluded that they were no good at speaking.

As we accumulate more patterns, we become more efficient, but that also inhibits our ability to adapt and grow. We may be efficient but not effective.

Understanding how the brain makes decisions, questioning and exploring, and seeking diverse perspectives are three possible approaches to avoid these traps. By some quirk of fate, probably just a random occurrence, those just happen to be the pillars of this book.

On the one hand, our brain is wired to create patterns and stories, and that ability is what allows us as a species to adapt to, and then function in, so many different situations. On the other hand, that same ability results in two deficits:

1. We sometimes reach false conclusions because we see patterns that do not actually exist.
2. Once we have established these patterns and stories, our brain filters out and distorts the data that doesn't fit the patterns we already developed.

The trouble is that once we have a script or habit, it takes on a life of its own and generates inertia of the mind.

This is true for our own scripts as individuals, and it's just as true for the scripts and stories we generate as a group or society. We've been talking about individual scripts and stories, but their application is even more widespread and universal. In fact, some of the stories that have allowed us, as individuals or groups, to thrive may also be leading us to destroy ourselves in the future unless we start understanding how they affect us today.[4] For example:

---

[3] Artificial Intelligence is no different. How many buy in to the story that AI is going to save the planet? How many others are saying that AI is going to destroy civilization? Could those stories be simplifications? Could they be examples of apophenia?

[4] While I do think that some of the patterns, stories, and scripts that were successful in the past are becoming counterproductive and might lead to us destroying ourselves in the future, this was actually put forward by Mihaly Csikszentmihalyi in his book *Creativity: Flow and the Psychology of Discovery and Invention*. He further explained that when a story becomes a rigid rule, it prevents us from responding to a changing world.

- We have had this story in the US that hard work results in success, and that if someone is not successful it's because they did not work hard enough. This story obscures system inequalities, which reduce opportunities for sections of society and can lead to frustration, disillusionment, and angst.
- We have had this story of the US as a melting pot, that each culture melds into a common homogeneous society. But this story also suppresses diversity and has often led to discrimination, reduced opportunities, and social disharmony.

Here is an example of a society-wide story that justifies certain scripts we all follow. This is a meme that many, if not most, in our society swear by.

The story determines the actions

It's a competitive world, it's survival of the fittest, get what you can when you can

(*image generated by ChatGPT*)

It's a competitive world; it's survival of the fittest; get what you can when you can.

"Survival of the fittest" is the catchphrase used for Darwin's theory of evolution. Organisms survive because they are better adapted to their environment than other organisms. Natural selection ensures that species that are well adapted survive; those that are not go extinct.

Darwin's theory of natural selection has been adapted to society as social Darwinism and is a foundation of capitalism. Survival of the fittest means that everyone should act in their own self-interest, and an invisible hand will pull all those actions together to advance the common good.

Think about what this means in the following situations and how following this story might determine how we would act:

- I have a large lunch, and the person across the table can't afford lunch.
- I'm taking a test for grades, and the person next to me probably has the right answer.
- I have some garbage, there isn't a trash can nearby, and no one is watching me.
- I'm hungry, and there are free apples on the table, but there are five apples and ten of us, and I'm right next to the table.
- My company produces and refines oil; prices are really high, and people are suffering; high prices are very profitable; we have the capacity to produce more oil although that would lower prices and profits this year.

Here is an alternative story:

An Alternative Story

Humans are a part as well as stewards of the world and thrive through mutual benefit and cooperation

(image generated by ChatGPT)

Humans are a part as well as stewards of the world and thrive through mutual benefit and cooperation. Yuval Noah Harari, in *Sapiens: A Brief History of Humankind*, maintains that the thing that has made *Homo sapiens* the dominant species is our ability to come together to solve problems and build solutions.

Many environmentalists, social justice advocates, humanists, and social entrepreneurs adopt this mindset. They would argue for increased cooperation and focus on long-term sustainability, a shift in power dynamics, and inclusion.

What does this mean in the same situations, and how might it determine how we act?

These different worldviews result in vastly different actions.

Which is reality? Which is right?

In fact, if we believe either story, that's our reality. Neither is reality; they are both stories. Remember, stories are simplifications that allow us to rapidly make sense of a situation and take action. If we fully believe either story, we make everyone who believes in the other story wrong. If we see that there are aspects to each story that are helpful, we are in a position to have dialogues with both sides, and we are able to have a more nuanced understanding of what is happening.

In the survival of the fittest story, it's hard to come to terms with the side of human nature that nurtures and supports. In the stewards of the world story, it's hard to understand why competition can benefit mankind, why wars have been so common throughout history, or why many entrepreneurs are so motivated by wealth.

Both are stories, and it's probably helpful to think of how each is useful in different domains.

- Which is likely to lead to sustainable or regenerative development?
- Which is likely to lead to winning in a competitive situation?
- Which is likely to lead to decreased emissions and pollution? (Or, even better, how could each lead to this result?)
- How is each likely to lead to new and better technology that supports the broader society?
- Which is likely to lead to a rising tide of wealth?
- Which is likely to lead to self-reliance and ownership of one's responsibilities?

For each of these questions, the story is going to dictate the solution. It's likely that for some of the situations the competitive survival of the fittest story will lead to a better outcome. For others, the we are all in this together story will result in better results. And considering any of the situations while keeping *both* stories in mind will often lead to even better outcomes than blind belief in either one would arrive at.

Here are other story pairs:

Illegal immigrants are flooding into the US and taking jobs away from citizens.	Our country was built by immigrants, and allowing more immigration is crucial to growth and prosperity.
Guns should be banned because there is too much violence.	The right to bear arms is guaranteed by the Constitution, and any restriction is taking away the rights of our citizens.
The billions and billions of dollars that we are pouring into Ukraine should be first going to support US citizens. Ukraine has had corrupt governments since they left the Soviet Union, and Ukraine is destined to lose anyhow.	The US is the defender of democracy, while Russia and Putin are trying to destroy it; we need to support Ukraine, or we will end up fighting Russia here. Plus, over 80 percent of the money we give Ukraine ends up being spent on US companies, so we really are not giving Ukraine nearly as much as it seems.

Stories are just simplifications that allow us to rapidly make sense of a situation and take action. As long as we accept a story, we don't have to think; we can just let our limbic system work autonomously without having to put the prefrontal cortex to work.

If we believe a story on one side:

1. Our reaction to those supporting the other side is likely to be limbic based: fight, flight, or freeze.
2. We are likely to ignore and discount any data or information that does not support our view.
3. We are likely to accept information that supports our view, even if it is not based on actual events or data.

Political leaders, authorities or thought leaders, social media personalities, news media, and advertisements and commercials are all bombarding us to act and think in certain ways. Each of them has an underlying story. Understanding what the story is, knowing that stories are just shortcuts, and exploring alternative stories gives us power.

The issues behind the stories above, and many more like them, are important problems that we are not solving:

- How should we be handling immigration?
- How do we reduce violence?
- How do we allocate resources?

Wouldn't it be wonderful if, instead of Saboteur-to-Saboteur conflict, we could make Sage-to-Sage connections? That would mean we could have meaningful, constructive discussions with people we disagree with.

Maybe we can start with the next generation. Maybe we can give them tools for critical thinking, creativity, collaboration, and perseverance by helping them recognize when they are operating from limbic mode and then how to move their thought processes to their prefrontal cortex.

We often tell students to look for sources, but it might be even more effective if we walked them through (and if we ourselves followed) this process:

1. Tell us what story this leader, article, post, video, or advertisement is trying to get us to believe, and what actions it would like us to take,
2. Come up with some alternative stories, then
3. Explore and investigate sources.

This process of questioning the story and exploring other possible stories is a key ingredient of critical thinking, but it's often ignored in an education system that seeks to give students the "right answer" so that they can get it right on the test.

Chapter 2 Review

This chapter introduced the concepts of scripts (rules, habits, common sense, heuristics) and stories (rationalizations, explanations), how our brains build scripts and stories, why they are advantageous for survival and efficiency, how they help us learn, and also how they can limit us.

We explored a few situations where stories and scripts might not bring out our best selves. Is it really in our best interest to flash a finger at some stranger who annoys us? When a leader or authority lulls us into their story in order to elicit some action, is that in our best interest, or might we be better off if we looked at the story, explored alternatives, and came to our own conclusions?

When I was having those "What did you do today?" conversations with my kids, we both were locked into our own stories and scripts. Neither of us made an effort to understand the others' story, and we were both frustrated by each other's scripts.

I think that if I were interacting with my teenage children today, I'd have many more tools to connect with them and be a better parent.

Most of us pass through most situations blissfully unaware that we are merely reacting. How do you know you are following a script? How do you know you are in a story? If you are in a story and script, how can you discern if it's beneficial or not?

That's what we will explore in the next chapter.

CHAPTER 3

Silencing Our Inner Critic

In chapter 2, we covered stories, scripts, habits, patterns, and rules in general, how they speed up our responses and also reduce the amount of hard thinking work we have to do when meeting up with situations similar to those we've seen before.

Scripts work in our limbic brains, so they get activated in hundredths of a second, and they also prevent us from critically thinking and being resourceful, just as the story "I can't" did.

We also covered what Phil Stutz calls Part X.

Part X is a running commentary that takes place in all of our brains, constantly criticizing. It's giving us a false dialog that keeps us from trying, changing, or growing. When we succumb to it, we get a short illusion of pain going away; when we develop powers to defeat it and try something new and grow, we get a sense of elation. Even with that elation, it keeps coming back, which gives us new demons to vanquish.

Part X is a story, and this chapter is going to explore how we can recognize when we are in a story or operating from a script, and then some of the ways we can exit into resourcefulness.

Part X is Phil Stutz's term; Shirzad Chamine calls this function of the brain Saboteurs. When our brain tells us stories that hold us back, the Saboteurs are active.

Saboteurs use the limbic system's inherent bias for finding danger to generate fear-based stories that limit us to limbic reactions to situations. The limbic brain is always judging, and Chamine calls the master Saboteur the Judge. The Judge has us badger ourselves for past mistakes or current shortcomings. It focuses on what is wrong with others and gets into inferior/superior comparisons. And it insists that outcomes are or will be bad. The Judge is abetted by accomplice Saboteurs, which we will examine in chapter 6.

Here is an example of how one person recognized and overcame her Part X or Saboteurs.

Roberta, who was in one of my classes, says that she has always felt obligated to follow the gender roles script when it comes to household chores. It's her job to scrub the bathroom, dust, do the laundry, cook the dinner, etc. Her husband goes to work. So does she. While she resented having to take on so much housework, she had no choice: the housework needed to be done, and both she and her husband expected it to be done by her.

What do you think are the stories and scripts that Roberta and her husband accepted? Were they helpful, or did they hold them back?

Roberta had a few options:

1. She could continue to do all the housework.
2. She could stop doing the housework and let the chips fall where they may.
3. She could tell her husband she wasn't going to do it anymore.
4. She could initiate a discussion with her husband on the subject of gender roles and housework.

How do you think Roberta's Part X reacted when she considered what to do? Part X is designed to attack any form of action we take, bringing us back to the known status quo, where it also attacks us for lack of action.

What Roberta accepted as reality was actually her Part X's story; it was a false dialog that kept her from trying, changing, or growing.

Roberta decided that her stories were not helpful. She made up her mind to move past them.

She initiated a conversation with her husband where they questioned their household roles. It turned out that he didn't accept the gender roles story either. They developed a new story, that it takes a team to make a house function and that no one has to do it by themselves. They have both found this new story very freeing, and Roberta reported that it's quite lovely to not have all the responsibilities on her shoulders.

In this chapter we will develop techniques to become aware of the stories and scripts we follow, and how we can start changing them by bypassing our Part X and Saboteurs.

As we learned, it's hard work, or heavy cognitive load, to build a story and piece together a response, but once we have a framework or a story, the response can be automatic without much conscious effort. That's why the human brain developed the ability to use scripts and stories.

Script/Story Benefits

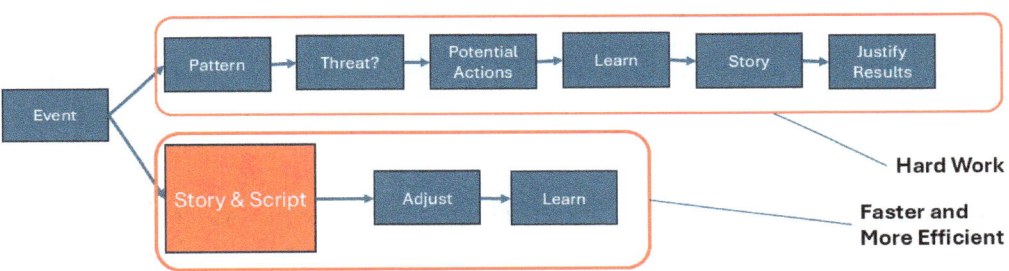

Story: mental framework for organizing knowledge **Script**: actions for routine activities

People often ask what the difference is between a script and a story.

> A **story** is a mental framework for organizing knowledge: dog-eat-dog world, every person for himself, housework is for women. Those are stories.

> A **script** is an action where you are fluent, where you don't have to use much cognitive load. We can think of scripts as actions for routine activities. Walking is a script. The conversation opener "How are you?" "Good, how are you?" is a script.

The story justifies the script, or you could say that the mental framework is what justifies the action.

Which comes first, the story or the action? There is no one answer; it depends.

- Sometimes we don't have to justify the action. We just act, and we don't have to think about it at all.
- Sometimes we act and then use the story to justify it. Maybe we acted without thinking, but then someone asks why we did that, so our brains use a story to justify what we just did.

- Sometimes we start with the story and then the story triggers the action. Advertising does this a lot. They might show a good-looking model enjoying life and using their product; they are hoping that story triggers us to buy what they are selling. Or maybe a student has a story that a teacher doesn't like them, and that triggers them to disrupt class or not pay attention.

Mihaly Csikszentmihalyi pointed out that many stories and scripts and rules were initially successful, but then they develop a persistence beyond their usefulness, and then they become rigid rules that actually inhibit our effectiveness and well-being.

Roberta's gender-specific roles is an example of a story and script that at one time may have been useful but whose persistence, for her family at least, had extended beyond its usefulness.

"Don't talk to strangers" is a story that works to keep children safe, but when those children go to college, everyone is a stranger. Keeping that story as a rigid rule is extending it beyond its usefulness.

You might have grown up in a family where disagreements escalated, possibly to violence. "Conflict is bad" would have been a useful story.

"Conflict is bad" would mean that maintaining peace and harmony are always the most important thing. The scripts resulting from the story might lead to procrastination or avoidance of situations that could cause conflict, or they might lead to passive-aggressive behavior, or always doing whatever other people want, even if it is wrong or causes high stress, instead of direct actions to relieve conflict.

Stories are always oversimplifications. Some conflicts really are bad. Sometimes constructive conflicts can lead to better solutions than either side could have created on their own. Sometimes they can lead to collaboration. Sometimes they are necessary to stop an even larger conflict. My former partner Farimah and I had many conflicts, and most of them led to solid outcomes that we would never have achieved if we had not engaged. But in every case, our Part X, our Saboteurs, our Judges were there telling us to avoid friction, to give in because the risk of a fight wasn't worth it.

How do you know you are in a story and following a script?

Most of the time, we are in a script. Whenever we react, whenever we don't need to pause, whenever we know what to do, we are in a script. And also, most of the time most of us aren't aware we are in a script.

Cornelia Walther, in her book *Technology, Social Change and Human Behavior*, pointed out that "like animals, we have evolved to decide fast with little information, as this is often a critical factor of survival."[1]

Stories and scripts aren't necessarily bad; they are what help us navigate through our days, to decide fast with little information or cognitive effort.

In the US, when we see someone, we don't have to think hard to say, "Hello, how are you?" Then they don't have to think about how they really are; they also follow a script with "Fine, and how are you?"

In Finland, one doesn't generally ask "How are you?" If you do ask "How are you?" it means you genuinely want to know about the person's health and feelings, and you are likely to get a quite detailed and lengthy answer.

Stories and scripts vary by culture, which sometimes results in misunderstandings with grave or sometimes funny consequences. Look up the HSBC video about eating eels, or follow this QR code:

Stories and scripts are beneficial when they work for us, and they are detrimental if they make us feel bad or prevent us from accomplishing what we desire.

I have this story about myself that I'm *very good* at a lot of things, and that I'm *not great* at anything. For me, that's motivating. It's a story that works for me because when I really think about it, it makes me happy. I can be proficient and enjoy lots of different activities, and I don't feel this burden that I have to be perfect.

If that story prompted me to think "I'm worthless, I really need to be great at something," then for me, the story would be limiting, and I would want to act in a different way or come up with a new story.

---

[1] Walther also said, "Although heuristics are useful shortcuts for everyday judgment calls, they can lead people to make decisions which are not only fast but incorrect, because as situations become more complicated, shortcuts based on simplification are prone to fail."

In other words, I've thought about and accepted this story. I'd encourage you to do this with your own scripts and stories, to question them:

- Does doing this make me happy?
- What is the story or reason I give myself for doing it?
- Do I enjoy this story and how it supports the way I act?

If it does bring happiness and enjoyment, that's great. If not, it's time to make a change.

Returning to Dr. Cornelia Walther,

> To influence decision-making processes, we must not only think about what we feed the brain, but also refine our awareness of how the different parts of the brain respond. Simply said—meta-thinking (thought about thought) is required to improve the outcomes of our thinking. If we are alert to errors in the thought process itself, we reduce the risk of irrational choices, although we may not be immune to *emotional corruption*.
>
> The point of departure for any endeavor in this direction is to admit that not just the minds of others, but also our own minds, are prone to mistakes. The subsequent step is to understand how these mistakes happen and how they feed our overall operating model.

To become conscious of whether we are in a story or acting out a script, we must learn to use meta-thinking, metacognition, thinking about thinking, or self-awareness.

Whenever you are doing something and you don't have to think about it, or it's really clear what you should be doing so that you don't even question it, that's a great indication that you are in a script.

And a lot of the time, that's good. The script and story behind the script are saving you time and effort and maybe even keeping you out of danger.

Recognizing that you are operating out of habit is one of the most important skills you can get out of this book, so let's spend more time on it. That starts with meta-thinking. With meta-thinking we can learn to question and improve the outcomes of our thinking.

Most people have no idea that they are in a script or story and that they can change the story or script, which would make them more flexible, better critical thinkers, or more persistent. In fact, most of us aren't even aware that there are alternatives to the inner dialog or stories we tell ourselves or that the actions we take are controllable and changeable. We just react to whatever our perception is.

Many people believe that the more homework kids do, the more they learn. Many believe that standardized tests are the best measure of a student's ability or a teacher's effectiveness. Do you think people who believe those are critically evaluating data about that? Do you think they realize that they are in a story and following a script, that their limbic system is inhibiting their prefrontal cortex from thinking critically or reassessing that position?

We do have a choice. You do not have to accept the story from your limbic reaction. You can write your own story.

I remember the first time I learned that I could control my reality. I was attending a self-improvement lecture, and the speaker said that it's not the event that triggers a reaction; the reaction is triggered by what is inside of our own heads.

The example she used was a traffic jam.

We all get stuck in traffic. Sometimes we start thinking "I really have to be somewhere else. This is wasting time. Can't these people move," etc. Then we start getting angry. Other times we are in traffic, and perhaps we are listening to music or thinking about something, and we barely notice it. It's not the traffic that is causing us to be angry, it's us.

Her revelation was that if we are aware we are getting angry, we can change our reaction.

Do we enjoy getting upset about a slow driver in front of us or being stuck in traffic? If we don't, through practice, we can learn to replace that anger reaction with a different reaction. "Let me listen to the radio and really concentrate on the music. Let me put on an audiobook and learn. Let me call someone and troubleshoot some issue."

I heard that, so the next time I was in a traffic jam, and I was starting to get anxious and angry, I just said to myself, "It's not the event that triggers the reaction, it's in my own control how I react, and I can enjoy this time whether or not I am in traffic." And it worked. It was like, "Oh My Gosh, that is so cool."

Just knowing that stories and scripts exist will probably have a profound influence on you. It certainly has with me and with others who have been through Mind-Shifting workshops. You'll start questioning, "Hmm, do I have to do this this way?" It will even help you working with others, when you ask yourself "Is this person operating under a different story than mine? How does that influence what she thinks and does?"

How do you know you are in a script? You're in a script and story most of the time.

- If you don't have to think about what you are doing, you are probably in a script.
- If you are doing something that you've done before, possibly many times before, you are probably in a script.
- If it is clear what you should do, or if you feel you *have* to do something a certain way, you are probably in a script.

Someone bumps into us, and we know we have to push back. Someone criticizes us, and we feel we have to criticize them. Somebody brings up one more alternative after we felt a matter was settled, and so we have to scold them for delaying. If you're seeing only one thing you can do, or you only see one good choice and one bad one, then you are probably operating in a script.

Stop and think for a second about things that you do.

- What is something you do where you feel *there is only one choice*?
  - Like me, do you feel that you have to get angry at a really slow driver in front of you?
  - When someone asks if you'll help out, do you feel you have to work extra hours even though you resent having to do it?
  - When you have too much on your plate, do you feel that you have to keep up with an overbooked schedule?
- What is something you do where you know that *there is only one good choice, and the alternative is horrible*?
  - Like Roberta, do you feel that you always have to clean the house, or it will be a complete mess?
  - Do you feel pressured to stay in a job you hate, or you will have crushing financial issues?
  - Do you feel you have to move for a partner, or that partner will resent you for the rest of their life?

Those are all scripts, or a story and a script.

Someone leaves the cabinet door open again, and you have to lecture them about it. And then they leave the door open again, and you lecture again. And again and again.[2] If you find that you are doing the same things over and over again and that the results aren't what you really want, you are probably operating in a script.

Someone is late for a meeting or class, and you always have the same response: you stop talking, look at your watch, and watch them take their seat before proceeding. If you haven't explored and really considered at least two or more alternatives, you're likely in a script. What are some other ways to respond to a person coming in late?

How do you get out of a story or script?

Maybe asking yourself a question is all you need to break out and come up with possibilities: "Perhaps there is another way" or "Maybe I *can* do this." Next time you're about to do something, ask yourself, "Did I consider alternatives?" or "What are three other ways I can possibly react?"

The driver in front of you is driving really slowly, and you can feel your irritation building. Maybe you can ask yourself, "What are three other ways I can react?"

You feel pressured to stay in a life-draining job because the alternative is to let everyone down. Can you ask yourself, "How can I give myself space to consider alternatives that might work?"

As you get stronger and over time, you'll have this self-awareness without even consciously thinking about it. That's basically what I've found, although I'm certainly still learning. In fact, I'm always in some class or reading some book on self-programming and coaching.

For me now, I can use self-awareness or meta-thought often when I'm not happy with my limbic option. I still often start to react impulsively, but I know enough not to immediately act. I wait a few seconds for my calming voice to say to myself, "Might there be another way to react?"

Recently my dad, who was 97 and had dementia, was in the hospital because he'd had a fall. The nursing assistant told me that he kept trying to get out of bed, that she was exhausted keeping him in bed, and that she was glad to see me so she could leave the room and I could keep him in bed. With me also, he kept trying to get out of bed, and I kept nudging him back. I was getting frustrated and angry. At some point it dawned on me: did I consider any alternatives, or was I just limbically reacting? In other words, I went meta.

---

[2] You are in a script because you are repeatedly telling them to close it. They are in a script because they are unthinkingly leaving the door open. And you're in a script together because your interactions are always the same. Knowing that you cannot force someone else to change, what are you going to do differently?

The aide had informed me that she was trying to keep him in bed. Why was I acting like that was the only alternative? What else could I do?

I chose to help him up, assist him as he walked with his walker, and then help him back into bed when he was done. I knew I could keep him from falling. He was happier getting up and walking, and after a few minutes was ready to go back to bed. In 10 minutes, he wanted to get up again, and I helped him up and around the room with his walker and then back into bed. This turned out to be a much better way of spending time with him than trying to keep him contained in bed.

When you are caring for someone with dementia, your goal becomes providing them with moments of joy. There is not much that they can do; they don't have a lot of control. But letting my dad get up when he wanted, helping him walk around, leading him back to bed when he got tired, those gave him moments of joy.

Keeping him in bed, that was just following the script and enduring through time.

Once you start asking these questions, you'll start seeing the same thing as well. Your first reaction will most likely be to follow the script, but you will also have a meta reaction, saying to yourself, "Is that the only way to react, or might a different reaction have better results?"

That's the whole crux of the growth mindset. You choose a goal, and you align your actions with that goal without judging yourself harshly based on results. And you keep moving. The more you practice that, the more it becomes a heuristic, a procedure permanently available in your limbic tool bag. You'll just get better and better at that.

And as you get better and better, you will help and coach others through that process, helping them ask these types of questions to replace their own limiting stories and scripts.

So far we've mentioned three types of situations where metacognition can tell you that you are in a script or story:

1. when you don't have to think about what you are doing,
2. when you are doing the same thing over and over again but not getting the results you want, and
3. when you see clearly that there is only one right answer or one thing to do, and anything else is wrong.

A fourth type of situation is when you are resisting doing something and you feel you have to force yourself to do it.

There are clearly unpleasant tasks that we all do. If you feel you have to do something and you are resisting doing it, why not question if this is just a story or script and that there might be other paths?

If you need a push to do something, the effort is not going to be sustained. Pushing ourselves can work over a very short term, but there is only so much energy we all have to push. It's much easier when we approach a task from a sense of exploration, curiosity, or play. "What could make this more fun?" "What reward can I give myself after completing this?" or "How does doing this contribute to my bigger goals?" are three possible questions we could ask ourselves to change from victim mode to a sense of ease and flow.

We can all remember from our childhoods things we loved doing and things we felt we *had* to do. Some of us loved playing an instrument. We couldn't wait to play, and practice was a joy. Others liked the *idea* of playing an instrument, but we really didn't enjoy the repetition of practicing. We either had to push ourselves or someone else needed to push us. Which ones practiced and played more and made real progress?

A lot of us face this with so many tasks. For me, going to the gym was a chore. I'd scroll social media. I'd call someone. I'd come up with some other task I needed to get done in order to postpone or avoid going to the gym. Then I'd feel really bad that I blew another chance to work out.

Realizing I often resist, I asked myself a question, "How does exercising contribute to my bigger goals?" The answer for me was not "losing weight." The answer was that after I exercise I feel really good about myself. That spurred me to the following routine:

1. I think about going to the gym and start to resist.
2. I think about how good I will feel after working out, and then the thought of getting up and doing it doesn't seem so bad while the reward seems worth it.
3. I get up and go to the gym.

It's not the situation, it's what is in our heads that triggers the reaction. The story of feeling good after working out was more compelling than the story of "Let me just do one more thing first."

When you are in a situation where you only see one way to do something, or one clearly good way and one clearly bad way, or when you have to force yourself to do something but you don't see any other way, or when you've done something many times but it doesn't seem to be doing any good, those are all times to step back and open up to other possibilities. Those are times when we may want to stop our scripts and rewrite our stories.

How do you stop a script or a story?

Interestingly, we can't just stop a script. We have to replace it with something else. We can't just say, "Stop saying 'I can't,' " "Stop procrastinating working out," or "Stop getting upset at your father." We need to replace it with something else, like "Perhaps I can," "What would make this fun?" or "How do I want to spend my time with my dad?"

Nobody has been able to lose weight by telling themselves to stop eating too much. That doesn't tend to work long term. You replace the "let me just eat this" story with one more compelling for you. Perhaps "what would I do if I wanted to eat healthily?" or another one that works for you. You *can* develop healthy habits, but you can't just not eat so much.

The specific things you resist and the questions that will put you into ease and flow are going to be different for different tasks and for each one of us. Here are some possible questions to break out of scripts and help rewrite stories.

- Am I in a script or habit?
- What would I love?
- What's the story I am telling myself?
- What are some alternatives that I haven't even thought of?
- What would make this more fun?
- What if I *could* do this?
- What can I do to make this better?
- What am I hiding from by doing this?
- What reward can I give myself after completing this?
- How does doing this contribute to my bigger goals?
- How else could I meet my goal?
- What can I do now that will make me happiest in an hour?

Try one or two of those right now. Start developing your new heuristic.

Think of something that you do instinctively and try asking one or more of the questions above.

Now think of something you feel you have to force yourself to do. Try another of the questions.

What changed?

Also, interestingly, very rarely can someone else replace a script for us. If I tell you "Perhaps you can" or "Whether you believe you can or cannot, you're right," you are more likely to feel my suggestion as a threat than to follow it. Remember, *you* said to yourself "Perhaps I can." Saying it to yourself was more powerful and more likely to work.

Only the person themselves can stop a script. No one can do it for you, and you can't do it for others, including your family, your coworkers, or your students.

While you can't change people, you might be able to coach them so they can change themselves. Many of the questions above can be rephrased to help others overcome their limbic reactions. And you'd be doing a service for others if you could coach them to ask these questions for and to themselves.

First, you would have to be in rapport with the other person, and second, what you say needs to be posed as *questions*, not *judgments*. Imagine the following question and then the follow-up question after a person said they couldn't do something:

> I understand. Just consider for a moment, if you could do that, what do you think you might do first?
>
> And then what would you do?

Contrast that with:

> Yes, you can. You just need to believe in yourself.

In the first dialog, you affirmed you heard them and merely suggested they follow an additional line of thought. It doesn't negate them and is less likely to trigger their amygdala to resist.

We have been talking about how to recognize when we are following a script or stuck in a story that is not particularly helpful.

Often, in addition to our Part X talking to us, we have negative *feelings*, such as fear or anxiety about starting something. Those are stories as well. Here is one way to rewrite the anxiety story.

Take out a sheet of paper or open up a new document.

List five things that you've accomplished that you originally found difficult, and maybe even thought about quitting, but did anyhow. Things that you can be proud of. These can be things like graduating, losing weight, achieving a good grade in a difficult course, cooking a special meal, something from a sport or interest, or some work-related accomplishment. Look back through your life and list five things that you've accomplished that you originally thought difficult or even impossible.

Once you have that list of five accomplishments, think back to your earlier years. What are some minor tasks at which you failed early in life and then ultimately succeeded? Maybe you can come up with a minimum of three: things that you might have achieved in school, or with a hobby or sport, or with your family or friends. List those too.

Hopefully, you now have about eight achievements that at one point you thought were very difficult, that you were tempted to give up on, but where you were ultimately successful.

Now just go back through your life one more time. What two additional tasks that you initially failed at, weren't good at, or were told you couldn't do did you proceed to accomplish anyhow?

The purpose of this exercise is that you can use your own past successes overcoming adversity to spur you on in whatever your current situation is. David Goggins, author of *Can't Hurt Me*, has a wonderful metaphor, **the emotional cookie jar**.

The fact is that persistence is like a muscle. The more times you've persisted and succeeded, the stronger you will be at persisting. When you remind yourself of how you've succeeded in the past, you inspire yourself to succeed in the present and future. This list of achievements is *your* emotional cookie jar.

How did Goggins change from an overweight, alcohol-fueled, minimum-wage deadbeat dad at 27 into the only member of the US Armed Forces to complete SEAL training, US Army Ranger School, and Air Force Tactical Air Controller training, a world-ranked ultra-marathoner, a best-selling author, and a sought-after motivational speaker?

Every time he attempted any of these feats, he had the same self-doubt, the same anxiety we all have when starting something difficult.

When he starts getting these negative messages, he looks at the list of all the times when he *has* persisted, his emotional cookie jar. He reminds himself of all the other times he has faced adversity and then triumphed. He remembers what it felt like to be tempted to give up, how he went on anyhow, what he overcame, and how he felt when he succeeded. And when he thinks about those, they inspire him to keep going; if he did it before, if he did it many times before, he can do it again. Then when he triumphs, that's yet another item he adds to his emotional cookie jar.

Silencing Our Inner Critic

If you're just reading and did not make that list, now that you know why I asked you to assemble the list, go and do it now.

Look over your list of achievements and answer these questions.

1. When you were doing those things, did you find them hard?
2. When you found them hard, were there times when you felt like giving up?
3. When you actually did succeed, how did you feel?
4. Isn't it great to know that there were times when things were really hard, and yet you were able to succeed anyhow?
5. Now imagine something you are finding difficult right now. Then look at this list. These were all times that you struggled, and yet you clearly have the ability to overcome challenges and succeed. You've faced challenges before. And you've won. That's what makes you *you*, and those are the things that you ended up really enjoying and remembering. How does that make you feel?
6. Don't you know you can do it again?

How do you think you can use this list the next time you are faced with a challenge and wondering if you can meet it?

The emotional cookie jar is a great technique for self-motivation. We can draw on our past successes and triumphs; we can draw on our own inspiration to push through our exhaustion, depression, pain, and misery.

When your brain tells you that you can't, you could say "I think I can."

Or you could also say to yourself that the feeling of being confused or uneasy or stressed is part of the process of growing. Go back and look at some of these awesome accomplishments on your list. Tap into them. Use them to inspire you and push you forward. Remember you're strong; you've done this before.

And for many of us, it's not just our own brain that initially tells us to stop or postpone. We have friends and family that also tell us we can't, or maybe they say "Just for tonight let's do something fun, you can always do this tomorrow," or whatever.

Tapping into our accomplishments is a powerful remedy for that negativity as well.

The emotional cookie jar is a technique we can and should use to help ourselves grow. And we can use it to help others as well. I've found this is helpful for kids as young as 10, although they often need more prompting to come up with their accomplishments, and it's very beneficial for teenagers to have an emotional cookie jar they can draw on.

Whenever we attempt to do something new, it's a challenge. We get anxious or fearful. To avoid those feelings, we develop a story that challenges are bad and should be avoided.

We often regard challenges as unwelcome. Yet I think we all find that our challenges in the past are what we had to go through so we could grow.

We'll always have challenges, and we'll always have that voice whenever we face a challenge that tells us we can't or shouldn't attempt it. That voice is what makes us anxious or fearful when we have a challenge, issue, obstacle, or problem. It will always be there, and left alone, it will always make us anxious.

Phil Stutz, Shirzad Chamine, Cornelia Walther, Jane McGonigal, Mihaly Csikszentmihalyi, and others all point out that it's overcoming those challenges, and especially overcoming those Saboteurs, that is the essence of progress and the essence of what makes us truly happy.

When we think back on the things we are most proud that we accomplished, we recognize every one of those was challenging, right? In every one, there were times when we could have stopped but we didn't.

That's a gift. And it's also an opportunity. We face a problem. We feel anxious. We continue anyhow. And we find out that in overcoming that problem we have made progress, and the process has made us happiest. The challenges that we face now and in the future are opportunities to grow.

What if we changed our frame? What if we thought of challenges as what we go through *so that* we can grow. We know that our feeling of anxiety or fear is based in our limbic system. It's our Part X or Saboteurs seeking to hold us back. We know that we don't have to let it stop us, and we could even let it motivate us.

You now have this list of accomplishments where you broke free of your anxiety, triumphed, and grew.

Think of a challenge you are facing right now. As you think of the challenge, try taking the position "This is a challenge that is helping me grow and develop new superpowers."

Many times, just reframing an issue as an opportunity to help you grow rather than as a difficult task you are forced to try will change it to a motivating challenge.

What if the next time you are challenged, when you start feeling anxious and are thinking of stopping, you think:

> Part of being challenged is also feeling anxious. Part of growing is being anxious, but just because I feel anxious doesn't mean I am in physical danger. Being anxious is part of growing—that's how we know we are becoming more powerful. We always get anxious when we are challenged. Feeling anxious is how we know we are growing.

We've talked about how the number one goal of the brain is survival, avoiding pain, suffering, and ultimately death. The limbic part of the brain can't distinguish something that is physically threatening from something that is just new. And so Part X or Saboteurs or the Judge go to work to increase the fear and anxiety, using stories that keep you fearful and telling you the lie that by not trying you are safe.

The fact is that with practically anything that is worthwhile, anything that is difficult, there is some point where you are confused, where you think you might not succeed. And left to the limbic parts of the brain, that confusion becomes anxiety or fear or "bad."

Psychologists talk about stress in general, but they also talk about distress and eustress. **Distress** is when stress stops us from doing. **Eustress** is when it helps us focus, and eustress can be used to motivate us to explore, innovate, and think. Stress, distress, and eustress are all stories; they are ways we can make sense of situations.

If you're anxious or confused, you're supposed to be. It's part of the process.

Imagine you are feeling stressed. Not pleasant? You can change your story so that confusion and low anxiety are a part of doing something worthwhile. They can also trigger curiosity, exploration, innovation, and learning.

Now imagine having that feeling and saying to yourself, "This is eustress. I can use it to motivate me to keep going. I live for these moments, and that's when I accomplish the most. Let's get going!" At different times we've all experienced a state where we were so focused on what we were doing that we lost all sense of time.

The situation is the situation, just like being in traffic is just being in traffic.

Our feelings about the situation are based on the story we are telling about the situation. Often, we can reframe a situation from causing distress to eustress just by recounting our past successes, by thinking about how challenges are what help us grow, or by anticipating how good we will feel when we have succeeded.

The situation is the situation. What changes is our story, which we can control.

When we reframe challenges as opportunities to grow, when we face an issue and pull out our emotional cookie jar of accomplishments to spur us on, we are changing the situation from distress to eustress.

It's always been interesting to me how many kids regard challenges in games and sports as motivational. They are eager to learn, improve, and triumph. Those same students regard tests as stressful. They are really the same thing: you do something, and you find out how well you did. Wouldn't it be great if they could reframe assessments in school to elicit that positive reaction?

One participant in a MindShifting class reported that she tended to procrastinate or become emotionally paralyzed whenever she thought about putting her desired outcomes into action. But when she asked herself, "How could this motivate me instead of paralyze me," she felt a surge of energy flowing through her. As she said about the experience, "The mind is so incredibly powerful and kind of sneaky."

Positive anticipation is a way to supercharge those goals as motivators, to imagine enjoying the benefits of achieving the result.

Psychologists use the term *anticipation* for imagining in the present something positive we expect to happen in the future. When we anticipate, we create memories of that imagined event in our brain. Research also shows that imagining good things ahead can make us feel better in the current moment.

Rachel Botsman, in her article "Why Anticipation Is a Powerful Creative Space," pointed out that anticipation strengthens and solidifies memories. The more you anticipate (and the more vividly you anticipate) something you desire to happen, the stronger your memory of the (future) occurrence will likely become, the more you will value the results, and the more likely you will be to move toward it occurring. The effect is even stronger when one shares that vision with others.

Many of us are able to articulate our goals. When we anticipate the results of achieving our goals, we in essence create memories of those imagined events in our brains.

Spiritual Alignment Coach Louise Taylor-Lopez, on her website, uses a similar technique, which she calls **Authentic Self-Activation**, as a way to bring remembered enjoyable experiences to life in the present. Let's do an exercise using Authentic Self-Activation.

Because it is often easier to perform Authentic Self-Activation on an existing experience, we will start with a past experience before using the technique to improve future performance. The added advantages are that the process is fun, and it tends to improve mood and reduce stress. You can use Authentic Self-Activation to perk up your mood the next time you are feeling a little down.

We will use food as our example. Imagine your favorite food or dish. As you imagine it, what are you sensing? Are you seeing it, smelling it, tasting it, hearing it, feeling it? Now make your perception of the food even more vivid and real by putting yourself into the experience.

- Is it hot or cold?
- How does it smell?
- Is your mouth watering?
- How does it look? What are the colors? What about the dish or serving plate?
- Can you pick it up? How are you going to eat it?
- How does it first taste? How does the taste change?
- Are you with others? What is their demeanor? How are you interacting with them?
- Where are you when you sense the food—out, in, at a restaurant, at home, at someone's house? What do the surroundings look like?

For most people, thinking about their favorite food this way, or thinking about any pleasurable experience with this level of sensory detail, makes it more real and is a very pleasant experience.

Now let's try the Authentic Self-Activation method, not with a past experience but as a way to prepare to succeed in a challenge. The more tangible we can imagine these results, the more we value the outcome and the more likely we will act on them and triumph.

Basic Anticipated Challenge

The difference between basic anticipation and clearly articulated anticipation is similar to the differences between the previous image and the following image. When we think about meeting a challenge, we generally have a hazy perception (like the previous image) of what the results will be. When we go through a formal effort to experience, see, hear, feel, smell, and taste the challenge and the results, we have a much more concrete perception, like the image below.

Clearly Articulated Positive Anticipation

There are at least (and probably more than) two different methodologies of positive anticipation. The **Success Anticipation Method** has the person facing the challenge clearly imagine themselves in the future and what it was like to succeed. The **SCORE Method** has the person facing the challenge clearly feel the difference between a situation where they were blocked and where they were resourceful, and then bring that resourcefulness over to the situation where they have traditionally been blocked.

Success Anticipation uses anticipating the enjoyment of the benefits as a motivational force. SCORE uses past successes as a guiding light to future success. Both are motivating. Try out both.

Here is the Success Anticipation Method.

Think of something challenging that you would like to do or accomplish.

Imagine that it is some time in the future, and you did it or accomplished it. Answer these questions:

- How does it feel to achieve this goal?
- What are you celebrating right now?
- What emotions are you experiencing in this moment of success?
- What are your surroundings now that you have achieved this?
- What are you saying to yourself about this achievement?
- What new opportunities has this accomplishment opened up for you?
- What new skills have you mastered in the process?
- There must have been times that you felt like stopping. What did the voices say to you to try to get you to stop?
- What did you do or say to yourself that kept you going?
- Who else is happy that you succeeded?
- How are you celebrating this success?
- What did you learn in the process?
- How did this success inspire others?
- Now imagine that you are talking to someone about this achievement and the process of going from where you are now in the present to that time in the future where you have succeeded and are talking to them. How are you describing that process to them?

Do you see the similarities between the Success Anticipation Method for something that you want to accomplish and the Authentic Self-Activation used on a pleasant remembered experience? They both create tangible memories in the brain.

Activating the senses to create a concrete scenario of success is a very powerful motivational technique. You may start out with a general sense of what you are trying to achieve. Asking yourself questions that involve seeing, feeling, hearing, and possibly even tasting or smelling what it is like to succeed, including the possible obstacles along the path, can make the goal more memorable and can prepare you both to start and to persist despite the effort of Part X and the Saboteurs.

You can also use these questions and the Success Anticipation technique with others to help them motivate themselves to meet their own challenges.[3] If you'd like to learn more about the application of positive anticipation, James R. Doty's book

---

[3] These questions are an effective and fun way to help another person motivate themselves. Perhaps you can ask them to write down their answers to these questions as they imagine themselves succeeding in something that challenges them.

Into the Magic Shop: A Neurosurgeon's Quest to Discover the Mysteries of the Brain and the Secrets of the Heart is a very readable place to start.

The SCORE method is described in *Tools for Dreamers: Strategies for Creativity and the Structure of Innovation* by Robert B. Dilts, Todd Epstein, and Robert W. Dilts. The acronym stands for

- **Symptoms** that indicate you are having a problem, such as feeling blocked,
- **Causes** of those symptoms, perhaps someone saying something that throws you off,
- **Outcomes,** or ways of being resourceful that you would prefer over the symptoms that you feel,
- **Resources** that you could use to remove the symptoms, and
- **Effects**, or the long-term outcome on your life, family, or community of being able to achieve the outcomes.

Dilts recommends using this method for recurring situations where you know that you get blocked. For example, if every time you have to publicly speak, you clam up, or if every time your partner asks or tells you to do something, you do it but feel you are being taken advantage of.

The SCORE Method is thus used in situations where you feel anxious every time they occur. And the purpose is that instead of feeling anxious when they occur in the future, you feel playful, curious, and resourceful. Remember the three-part diagram of the brain. When the limbic system senses danger, it both embarks on a fight, flight, or freeze action and also inhibits the prefrontal cortex from being resourceful. SCORE restores the prefrontal cortex to its resourceful state by tapping into the sense of fun, play, and curiosity you experience when you really are resourceful.

In this method, Dilts uses an anchor to provoke resourcefulness. An anchor is a stimulus (which could be a sound, word, image, smell, taste, or physical sensation) that can be linked to a specific emotion or behavior. When the stimulus occurs, it triggers the emotion or behavior. In everyday life, a song may trigger an emotion or memory. For many of us, taking a deep breath and letting it out slowly can be an anchor that provokes a feeling of calm.

Our phone's alarm might be an anchor that provokes us to look at our calendar to see what we need to do next. A runner might visualize themselves crossing the finish line feeling strong and victorious to spur them on in a race. A student might condition themselves to listen to a specific piece of music to calm themselves before a test.

Coming up with an anchor to trigger resourcefulness is a key part of the SCORE Method. The anchor could be a word, a touch, a way of breathing, looking at something, or a discreet action like tapping a finger or looking at a watch.

For me, the challenge I first used was interruptions by my wife. I tend to work on tasks using my computer, where I need an hour or two of uninterrupted time. Imagine I am working, concentrating, in a state of flow, and I hear my wife from two rooms over say, "Why did you leave this here?" I don't know what "this" is, I don't know where "here" is, and I don't even know if I was the person who left it. What I do know is that it's going to take quite a while to bring my thought processes back to where I was when I was making great progress on my task.

I have never been able to feel resourceful in that type of situation. I tense up. I get anxious. I worry if I'll be able to get back into the flow again. I get angry at my wife for interrupting.

This occurs at least a few times a week. I feel frustrated. It takes me away from the problem I'm working on, and it often takes quite a while before I can get back to my thought process. What I want is to stay resourceful and be able to handle the interruption while not losing track of where I am in solving the problem I am working on. And never mind that perhaps I should learn not to leave my things in random places around the house. As the reader, you should clearly be taking my side in this.

Here is how I used SCORE:

Symptoms: I reconstructed what it feels like to be interrupted.

Cause: I knew this occurs when I am concentrating on something and my wife interrupts.

Outcomes: I decided that I would like to feel playful and perhaps curious, just like when I am focusing on a fun challenge.

Resources: I generated the feeling of solving a fun puzzle and anchored that feeling by putting my hand on my shoulder and smiling.

Effects: I imagined my wife interrupting me. I put my hand on my shoulder, and that triggered a light and resourceful feeling. In that fun, curious state, I felt able to come up with better responses than I would have from frustration or anger.

That certainly beats staying angry!

Try this.

Think of some challenging situation that occurs where you feel blocked, but you want to remain resourceful: perhaps a type of interaction in some interpersonal relationship that causes you to feel blocked.

1. Identify when, in trying to accomplish this challenge, you feel blocked. This is what Dilts calls "identifying the symptoms" of the problem state. What is the feeling that you would like to change?
2. Explore the causes of the symptoms. What triggers that feeling of being stuck? What is it that you do, hear, say, or see that when you sense it, you get that feeling of being stuck? What does that feel like?
3. How would you like to feel when that situation occurs, the one that triggers the stuck or blocked reaction?
4. When have you felt that way before? What is the environment or trigger that then results in you feeling resourceful? What could be an anchor that would then cause you to feel that?
5. Remember a time when you wanted to meet the challenge, but you were blocked. Play the scene as if it were a movie or video and stop it right before you feel blocked. Use the anchor to stay in a resourceful state.
6. Come up with one alternative you could have done if you had been in that desired state. Then come up with at least two more alternatives while you are still in this state of resourcefulness.
7. Rewind the tape back to the beginning, and at the moment you would ordinarily feel blocked, invoke the anchor and cycle through those three alternatives.
8. Imagine a situation in the future when you would need that resourcefulness. Can you use the anchor in that situation? When you are in that situation and you use the anchor, can you wonder, "That's interesting. What could I do to take care of this in a new way?" How do you feel in those situations?

In order to be resourceful, you have to be able to get into a frame of mind where you can come up with alternatives, and generally this would be a playful or a curious state of mind. You are blocked because some trigger generates a story or script that puts you into an anxious or noncreative mindset. SCORE is a method for MindShifting by imagining other situations where you have been resourceful, using an anchor to prompt that state of mind, testing it out with past situations where you were blocked, and testing and reinforcing it with some future interaction where you would normally be blocked.

In my case, where my wife was interrupting my work, the anchor I used was a deep breath, putting my hand on my shoulder, and smiling. This triggered a sense of play. The three alternatives I came up with from that sense of play were:

1. Doing a quick giggle and saying, "Be there in five minutes."
2. Saying, "Rosie left it there. Just leave it and I'll put it away before lunch."[4]
3. Saying, "I left it there because I need it in an hour. Just leave it, and I promise it will be gone this evening."

Often when a person approaches a project with trepidation, they are feeling some combination of overwhelm, lack of confidence, and fear about the future. The temptation is to push themselves or analyze what they should do, neither of which works in the long term. SCORE promotes action instead of analysis, provides momentum, lowers the energy needed to activate or start, and increases focus.

Now try using these eight questions to help someone else.

Let's say you are afraid of flying, yet you need to fly to some city to speak at a conference. There are many techniques you could use to overcome anxiety and fly there anyhow:

- When you hear that voice saying "I can't fly," you might respond with "Perhaps I can."
- You could take out your emotional cookie jar of past accomplishments to help realize that this is just one more challenge that you are capable of overcoming.
- You could anticipate the joy you will feel after making the speech and the effect of others appreciating what you have to share.
- You could imagine previous experiences where you've been resourceful and anticipate using that playful feeling to replace your fear of flying.

The Next Step is another technique you could use to reduce anxiety and stress while increasing the likelihood of acting and succeeding.

In The Next Step, instead of brooding about a daunting responsibility or endeavor, you think about and commit to only the next step.

Let's take that person who is afraid of flying.

Using this method, they would first imagine a person who is *not* afraid of flying. Then they would list the steps that person might take leading up to sitting in the plane when it is taking off.

1. They would make a flight reservation.
2. The day before, they would pack their bags.

---

[4] Rosie is our daughter, and she hasn't lived with us in over 15 years. While this is definitely a playful response, it didn't work.

3. They would take transportation to the airport to arrive two hours before the flight.
4. They would check in to the flight at the airport.
5. They would go through security.
6. They would travel to the gate.
7. They would pass through boarding, showing their ticket.
8. They would pass through the walkway to the plane.
9. They would get on the airplane.
10. They would find their seat and sit down.
11. They would buckle their seatbelt.
12. They would stay seated after the announcement that the doors were about to close.

Deciding to travel might mean to decide on taking all those steps. But what if you only committed to do The Next Step. If you make a flight reservation, you could still decide not to fly. If you pack up your bags, you could still decide not to fly. At each action, up until after step 12, you could commit to doing that next act but reserve the right to back out.

This is what Tammie, a good friend of mine, did when she was asked to speak at the White House on game-based learning. She was based in Spokane, Washington, which meant she needed to fly to Seattle and then take another flight to Washington, DC, and then back. She felt tremendous pride and honor to be asked to speak to the Department of Education and other educators, but her limbic system, her Saboteurs, were stoking her fear of flying, and no amount of reasoning or desire could quiet them.

What did she do?

She decided that she could book her flight knowing that she could still back out. And so she booked her flight. The day before, she could pack her bags, knowing she could still back out. And so she packed her bags. She committed to one step at a time until she was sitting in her seat in the airplane. When she got to step 12 and they announced that the doors were closing, she said to herself, "Well, I've come this far, I'll just stay in my seat." She made it to Washington. She spoke. Everyone loved her presentation. She flew back. And she has now used that same technique other times her Saboteurs were in force, listing out the different actions and only committing to the next step.

If a person was anxious about proceeding with some task or challenge, and they wanted to use The Next Step method, they would

1. Write down or imagine all the steps that would be involved in completing the task and put them in sequence. They might consider doing this with someone else to make sure they included all the steps.
2. They would commit to doing just the next step.
3. They would actually do that step.
4. They would allow themselves to celebrate and feel good about completing that step.
5. When it came time for the next step, they would commit to doing that one step.
6. When that was complete, they would allow themselves to celebrate and feel good about completing that step.
7. And so on, until they either felt that they could complete the rest of the task, stopped, or completed the challenge.

More often than not, just starting is all one needs to continue to completion.

Chapter 3 Review

In each of these methods that have been covered, overcoming anxiety or fear or procrastination starts with knowing when you are stuck.

What are some of the things your Saboteurs do that stop you, limit you, or tell you to give up? Do they include any of the following?

- I don't have the time
- I don't have the knowledge
- I'm too old or too young
- I know it isn't going to work
- It's too hard
- If I failed it would be a disaster
- What can one person do?
- I have to do this myself
- These meetings are always a waste of time
- This is going to take too long
- People are going to laugh at me (or get angry at me)
- I never have any money left at the end of the month

Can you write down a few that really affect you?

You have a choice. You do not have to accept what your Saboteurs are telling you.

Here is a list of ways we have covered that can work to counteract those Saboteurs:

- Perhaps I can.
- I can take care of this right now.
- Am I in a script or habit?
- What would I love?
- What is the story I am telling myself?
- Challenges help me grow.
- This is eustress.
- That's exactly how I am supposed to feel when I try something new.
- Emotional cookie jar.
- Look at how great I'll feel when I've succeeded (which can be enhanced with the positive anticipation questions).
- The Dilts SCORE method.
- I only have to take the next step, then I can reevaluate.

All these techniques take a distress challenge and convert it to eustress. Instead of stress debilitating us, MindShifting turns stress into a motivational force.

The truth is we will always face challenges. Whenever we face a challenge, our Part X and our Saboteurs will always induce fear and anxiety about those challenges.

On the flip side, our greatest moments of happiness are when we proceed anyhow, and all our greatest achievements have been when we have found ways to vanquish those negative voices.

Roberta overcame her Saboteurs and initiated a conversation with her husband about gender roles. David Goggins was able to overcome years of sloth to become an elite athlete and sought-after motivational speaker. My friend Tammie was able to get on a cross-country flight and talk at the White House.

We all have the capability to recognize and overcome our Saboteurs, just like they have. We will dive into how and why in the next chapter.

CHAPTER 4

---※---

Mastering Our Mind

Sandra often feels overwhelmed, and when she feels that way, she tells herself she is too tired or too busy. This means whatever she is working on or doing, she just stops and rests. Now that she is familiar with the concepts of stories and scripts, she is aware that these reactions have often been the result of her Saboteurs or her Part X; they have stopped her from doing things that were important to her and that she would have enjoyed.

But not anymore.

In this chapter we are going deeper into cognitive science to better understand what happens in the brain when we transition from limbic decision-making to accessing the resourcefulness of the prefrontal cortex. This will give you a better understanding of why scripts and stories work and also why the types of techniques that give us all more mind control (like the ones in the first three chapters) work.

You are going to learn the mechanism behind quieting and recovering from Saboteur thoughts and actions, and then how to engage your resourceful mind so that your actions align more with your values and what gives you joy.

If you pay attention and practice, you might also find techniques to help others be more resourceful as well.

Rodolfo Llinás's *I of the Vortex: From Neurons to Self* examines the physics, chemistry, and biology of the neurons and the brain.

Our senses send our brain 11 million bits of information per second. Our conscious minds can handle only 40–50 bits per second. Which bits get prioritized and get through?

The brain prioritizes information that is helpful for survival. Our brains are capable of taking in a small bit of information and quickly directing the body to counteract any danger. It can do this because it acts as a reality emulator; the brain is basically a dreaming storytelling machine that constructs virtual models of the real world, sometimes modifies them through information, and initiates actions from predictions based on those models.

Charan Ranganath, in *Why We Remember: Unlocking Memory's Power to Hold On to What Matters*, adds that our brains discard what is not essential for our survival so that we can prioritize the information that is. Furthermore, memory is imagined; "the peculiar way in which we form memories can lead us to stray far from reality."

> We do not simply replay a past event, but use a small amount of context and retrieved information as a starting point to imagine how the past could have been. We put together a story on the fly, based on our personal and cultural experiences, and tack on those retrieved details to flesh out the story.
>
> Memories are neither false nor true—they are constructed in the moment, reflecting both fragments of what actually transpired in the past and the biases, motivations, and cues that we have around us in the present.

From an evolutionary standpoint, it doesn't matter if the concept of the world, or even the predictions, are accurate. They have to be *helpful* in those situations that threaten survival.

The brain, as covered earlier, is primarily focused on survival. It needs to take in a small bit of information to act quickly. It's developed the ability to learn fast, to use existing stories and skills to enact knee-jerk reactions or scripts, and then to use those stories to justify and reinforce those actions.

We spent a good deal of time on stories and scripts that hold us back from taking thoughtful action, and at least 12 different methods we can use to break us out of those stories and scripts.

The diagram below shows how the brain operates most of the time. You might recognize the three circles from the earlier simpler model of the brain: heuristics, emotional, and analytics.

Most of the time, something happens, we have a story and script about what we need to do, and we do it.

The default way of thinking

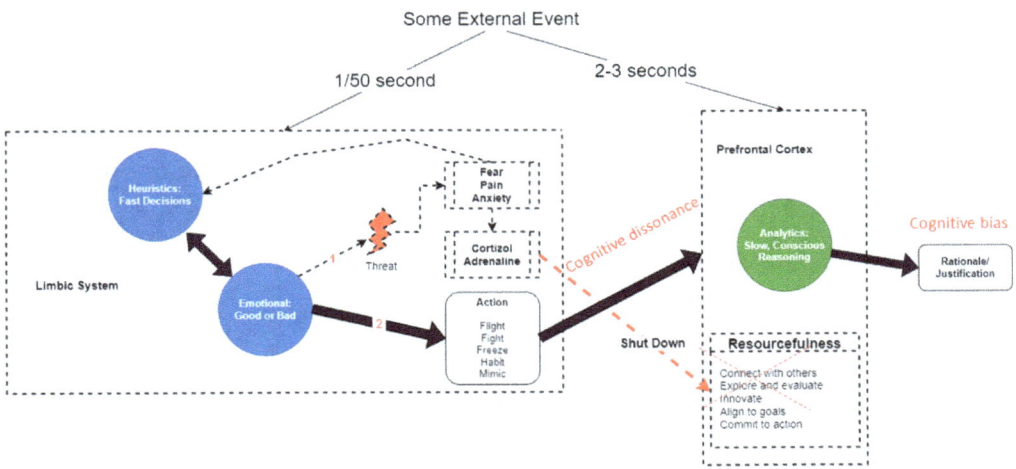

We've already explored that the heuristic and emotional parts of the brain are located in the limbic system, which acts quickly, and that consciousness, critical thinking, and creativity reside primarily in the prefrontal cortex, which acts a lot more slowly. By default, our limbic system comes up with potential actions and makes decisions to do something, react a certain way, say something, or maybe buy something. The limbic system makes its determination based on our biology and how we are conditioned to react.

Our conscious-thinking parts of the brain then create a rationale or justification for whatever decisions or actions we are taking.

The prefrontal cortex *can be* where we are resourceful. When activated, it can allow us to connect with others, explore and evaluate information, innovate, align actions to our goals, and focus us on some plan of action.

What happens when someone challenges that limbic action or the story behind it? That information, feedback, suggestion, or criticism is interpreted by the limbic brain as an attack. Attacks or threats result in the release of cortisol and adrenaline, which then focus the body's and brain's resources on the actions that have already been decided and shut down our abilities to think critically, take in new information, be resourceful, or question our scripts and stories. We then double down on the actions we've already decided upon, and we react with fight, flight, or freeze types of responses to the feedback.

This happens to all of us.

One teacher told the story about a teenager who had been bothering another teen. It was clear that the student had said some mean things to the other student and had really hurt them. The teacher took the teen aside and described how their words and actions were problematic. Do you think that student took in the feedback, came up with a plan to make things right, and thanked the teacher?

No, the student's reaction was to defend their behavior and make excuses. That doesn't have to be the end of the story though. As we will see later, it is possible to interrupt the emotional limbic mind and tap into the Sage exploratory powers to become aware of actions and their effect on others.

Why do we respond to criticism so defensively?

Because our brains are primed to develop conclusions on small amounts of data and shut down our prefrontal cortex, which could conceivably reassess our limbic decisions. We are prone to fight any suggestions counter to our conclusions. We humans are subject to a number of biases or thinking errors. When we know about them and recognize when they happen, we are more able to overcome them.

Cognitive dissonance is when we say we believe some things but then our actions do not align with those beliefs.[1] We say we believe in conservation, and yet we drive places we could easily walk to, for example. We say we want our students or employees to be open to experimentation, to try new things, to not be afraid of failing. And yet we grade and judge them so that if they are not perfect, they get points taken away or they are punished. Compliance is what is rewarded, and non-compliance is generally punished. What we measure, reward, and punish takes precedence over what we say.

Here are more examples of cognitive dissonance:

- You say you want to eat healthy, but then you eat junk foods.
- A male says he believes in equality of the sexes but then doesn't share household labor.
- A student says they want to do well but then has trouble focusing because they don't go to sleep at a reasonable hour, then justifies that they can catch up sometime in the future.
- A student who wants to be regarded as honest cheats on a test, justifying it as everyone is doing it.

---

[1] It's a good thing we live in a political system where our politicians do not embody cognitive dissonance. They never say one thing and then act in a completely opposite way, right?

- A teacher who dislikes busywork for students still assigns it, perhaps justifying it as that's what everyone is doing.
- A superintendent acknowledges the importance of the whole child and yet cuts arts and sports, justifying it through the need to improve test scores.
- A worker says they want to be trusted at work and then calls in sick so that they do not have to use a vacation day to do some errand.

Todd Rose, in *Collective Illusions: Conformity, Complicity, and the Science of Why We Make Bad Decisions*, explains how our minds end up justifying our cognitively dissonant actions.

> Cognitive dissonance can push us into lying to ourselves in order to feel less conflicted. As what we objectively know to be true clashes with what we feel or want to be true, an internal battle ensues between our beliefs and our behaviors. And more often than not, if we have already done something that conflicts with our values, then we instinctively adjust where we can. We resolve the discomfort by nudging our beliefs in one direction or another in order to feel more aligned.

Cognitive dissonance gets resolved by disregarding data rather than changing assumptions, beliefs, or methods—unless we are really good at honest self-awareness or metacognition.

A **cognitive bias** is a systemic error in thinking, and it results from our brain's efforts to simplify this incredibly complex world we live in. There are many types of cognitive biases.

Earlier, we touched on one cognitive bias, confirmation bias. Confirmation bias means that information that confirms what we already "know" gets noticed and processed, but we don't fully take in new data that might contradict what we believe is true. Our unconscious parts of the brain are blocking any analysis that the conscious brain would perform.

Dr. Ranganath points out,

> When we remember, we're like detectives, trying to solve a mystery by piecing together a narrative from a limited set of clues. A detective can build a case based on an understanding of the killer's motive, which can be helpful, but it can also lead to biases. In a similar vein, when we remember events, motive can exert a powerful explanatory role, helping us make sense of what occurred.
>
> Assumptions about people's motivations can also fuel our imagination, leading us to fill in the blanks about events in ways that distort our narratives of what happened.

Another factor that can bias our memories is that our own goals and motivations affect how we reconstruct an event. I'm often asked, "How is it that two people can experience the same event together and yet recall it so differently?" To quote Ben Kenobi from *Star Wars*, "Many of the truths we cling to depend greatly on our own point of view." People's different goals, emotions, and beliefs lead them to interpret an event from particular perspectives, and those perspectives will also shape how they reconstruct that event later on.

Let's say you believe a certain person is lazy. As you observe what this person does, whenever that person is late, makes a mistake, or doesn't measure up, your brain will use that as confirmation that the person is lazy. And every time that person does something well, your brain won't even notice. It's all unconscious.

People who believe Fox News is biased will look at stories that Fox reports that run counter to their beliefs as proof of bias. And people who believe that the *New York Times* or CNBC is biased look at stories that run counter to *their* beliefs as proof that the liberal media is biased.

Let's say I take a sip of wine. If I believe that bottle of wine costs $80, I am going to be inclined to regard it as tasting really good. If you were to tell me that the wine costs $10, I would be more likely to say that the wine does not taste good. Even with years of learning about wines, my internal story that expensive wines taste better biases my judgment.

Confirmation bias is a form of following a script and believing a story. Confirmation bias makes us less willing to accept others' ideas, and it rules out creativity, innovation, and diversity.

That's a good part of the reason that we primarily use our analytic reasoning to rationalize the decisions and actions we've heuristically devised and emotionally bought.

Here are some examples of cognitive bias, when people ignore "facts" that contradict what they believe to be true (**disconfirming evidence**) or when people make up connections that do not exist (apophenia, which we learned about in chapter 2):

- **Negative Bias**: the tendency to give more weight and attention to negative news than to positive news. For example, although statistics show a reduction of poverty rates compared to the past, people believe that development is stalled or worsening; the case is similar for wars and violence.
- **Teacher Bias**: A student dislikes a particular teacher and interprets all their actions negatively. A neutral comment by the teacher might be seen as passive-aggressive, confirming the student's negative perception.

- **Gifted Label Bias**: A person believes another person is gifted (belief) and focuses on their strengths, overlooking areas needing improvement (disconfirming evidence). They might downplay occasional struggles as "off days."
- **Teaching Method Bias**: A teacher prefers a specific teaching method (belief) and dismisses alternative approaches (disconfirming evidence). They might view student struggles with their preferred method as a lack of effort, not a mismatch in styles.
- **Discipline Bias:** A school district prioritizes a specific discipline approach (e.g., suspensions) (belief) and dismisses alternative methods like restorative justice (disconfirming evidence). They might view data showing a decrease in suspensions for schools with restorative justice initiatives as a flaw in the new approach rather than a sign that discipline problems are decreasing.
- **Apophenia**: A person is regarded as rude for not properly greeting another person, when the cause may have been that they did not see them, were deep in thought, or some other cause not related to being mean.
- **Bandwagon Effect**: the inclination to believe/do certain things because many other people believe/do so. People tend to walk the way of least mental resistance, and thinking for yourself means active effort.
- **Affinity Bias**: our attraction to working with people who look and think like us. It tricks us into believing that competent employees and great ideas are always objectively measured.

Cognitive dissonance and biases are a direct result of our brains' attempts to rapidly make sense of the world. They are all limbic reactions.

In the words of Dr. Cornelia Walther, "Heuristics are mental shortcuts to automate, and thereby accelerate decision-making, a necessary survival strategy in view of the limited capacities of the human brain, which needs to cope with and react to an abundant number of external stimuli. A heuristic that consistently leads to an erroneous decision is called a bias. Bias is the disproportionate weight given in favor of or against an idea, person, or thing. It may be innate or learned. Awareness to inbuilt defaults enables us to overcome them, and, consequently, change."

Our brains' inbuilt defaults, as we've discussed, are optimized around

1. Survival. Obviously, if something is threatening our life and we don't react, we don't live and we don't reproduce. Survival means building routines or skills where we don't have to think and that we can deploy quickly. The limbic systems are so much faster than the prefrontal cortex.

2. Conservation of energy. Our brains are about 2 percent of our mass and already consume about 20 percent of our energy. They are designed for efficiency, to reduce the amount of thinking and also to reduce reaction time by relying on things we already know how to do.
3. Blending in or mimicking others. We are social animals. We try to blend in, we learn from each other, and we form organizations that are capable of collaborating and building great works.

Those priorities result in the types of actions that we can do without having to do much cognitive work: flight, fight, freeze, habits (what we know how to do well), or mimicking (copying what others in our tribe are doing).

Imagine:

- A person is doing something from habit, or maybe because everyone else is doing it. Then somebody criticizes them.
- They need somebody to do something, but that person is late or doesn't do a good job.
- Some car cuts in front of them.
- They are running late.
- They are getting ready to leave and someone gives them some new task to complete.

The default reaction is not "Yay! Here is a fun challenge." Their reactions are just as ours are by default. Their brain releases the fear hormones, which shut down their prefrontal cortex. They lose the ability to connect, listen, evaluate, innovate, or align to their goals. When cortisol or adrenaline are released, any direct advice we offer, or any direct advice that others offer us, is ignored and wasted, right?

JoAnn was a participant in a MindShifting class and related an instance from the previous weekend. She and her significant other were going to paint their master bedroom and bathroom on Saturday. On Saturday morning, the SO mentioned that they were also going to paint the entire basement and all the rooms on the second floor.

No, her reaction was not "Yay! This is a fun challenge." It was "Why didn't he tell me this in the first place? This is going to take forever with only two people. We should have hired a crew to do this. We will never finish this during the weekend, and on top of that, any chance of relaxing has just been blown."

That's the default modus operandi of all our brains.

Contrast that with how we think when we are in a playful and curious mindset.

How we think when we are resourceful

We all have the ability to be incredibly resourceful. In these cases, we approach situations with a feeling of curiosity, play, or exploration, and the brain unleashes both joy and the ability to think creatively and critically through the release of the happy hormones serotonin, dopamine, oxytocin, and endorphins. The happy hormones amplify our prefrontal cortex's ability to be resourceful with the five powers that we will dive into momentarily.

Often, when we see an attractive opportunity, or are confident that we can meet some challenge, we are more resourceful. When we feel pressured, though, we are less likely to react this way, such as when there is a meaningful reward or punishment for some action or result.

When we see opportunity, when we are really coming up with effective actions, we are thinking more on these lines:

Something happens, and we see it as an opportunity (opportunity bolt) instead of a threat. Our mindset is playful, curious, and exploratory. We get excited from the various happy hormones that are released (serotonin, dopamine, oxytocin, and endorphins).

These hormones activate and engage our prefrontal cortex. In that mode, we really do empathize and listen to others, we explore relevant information and analyze it, we apply our creative thinking to innovate, we align possible actions to our goals, and we enthusiastically commit to some action.

Shirzad Chamine calls these the five powers of our minds when we are in creative or Sage mode. We start with a feeling of curiosity, play, and a sense of exploration to

1. Connect with others
2. Explore and evaluate what is happening

3. Collaboratively come up with different things we could do
4. Focus on things that are important to us and align to our goals and vision
5. Go into action with a commitment to overcome and go around and through obstacles

Notice the thick, solid black line labeled with the number 2 running back and forth between the limbic and prefrontal cortex systems. The proposed actions of our Sage minds still go through the emotional good/bad evaluation (as you see, this arrow goes two ways), but not from fear, more from opportunity, and when a potential action doesn't make sense, we don't beat ourselves up. We adjust to what we perceive as new opportunities and continue to go through the process.

When we think this way, we generally feel engaged and empowered.

We've all experienced this. And remember psychiatrist/therapist Phil Stutz observed that what makes us happiest is when we are in the process of creating something under the motivating pressure of eustress. This feeling is what psychologist Mihaly Csikszentmihalyi called flow.

When we feel this way, we are more resourceful, more resilient, more collaborative, more willing to work harder, and more likely to persist. Wouldn't we want to feel that way more often?

Cognitive scientists have looked at when we are likely to be in a state of flow, and it's a combination of both the challenge we are facing and our own competence and *feelings* of competence.

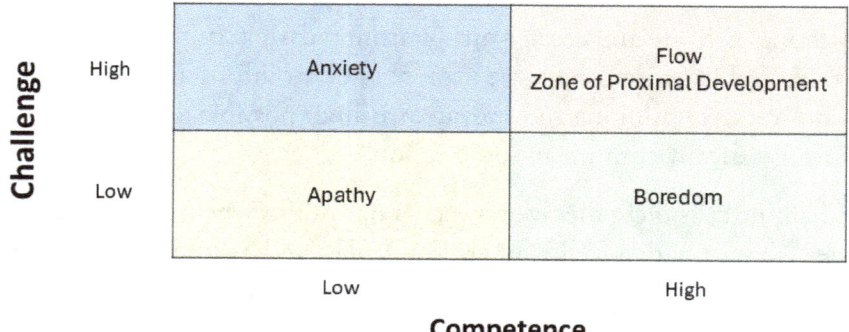

In the top left, when there is a challenge that we don't feel we can necessarily meet, we feel fear or anxiety. Our limbic systems tend to fight, flee, or freeze, or sometimes follow the crowd. For someone who does not feel confident speaking in front of crowds, public speaking might be a good example.

When there is no challenge and we don't have much proficiency, we are apathetic and unengaged (lower left). We will often procrastinate or freeze. Sometimes we finish a project only to find out there is a ream of unfamiliar paperwork to fill out. That's a task that many of us approach with apathy.

When there is very little challenge but we have a high degree of competence (lower right), we go into auto-pilot, and we are often bored. That's when we are mindlessly following habits or scripts or just doing what everyone else is doing. Someone proficient with computers might find repetitive data entry tasks extremely boring, or a student who has already mastered material might find practice worksheets boring.

And when there is a eustress challenge (upper right), we think we can be successful, although we aren't completely sure, and we have a commensurate degree of competence. In this quadrant, we can experience what Csikszentmihalyi would call flow, and we are in what Lev Vygotsky would call a zone of proximal development.[2] We are a little outside our comfort zone but not so much that we feel threatened. We all probably find flow in our leisure activities because we choose them based on where we feel we have confidence and yet are being challenged.

Any stimulus that is perceived with anxiety, apathy, or boredom gets processed by the limbic parts of the brain. Only when we perceive a stimulus as high challenge/high competence do we engage our prefrontal cortex and gain access to our resourcefulness and resilience.

A task is a task. Our brains develop the story that puts a task into a quadrant. We may regard a task as fitting into a particular quadrant. But we can also reprogram our brains so that more of the tasks we perform end up in that top right quadrant. That's what we do when using any of the 13 techniques in the last chapter: "Perhaps I can" is an attempt to move a situation from Anxiety to Flow, "What would I love?" "What would make this more fun?" or "Look at how great I'll feel when

---

[2] Lev Vygotsky (1896–1934) was a Russian psychologist who was the foundation for much of the research and theory of cognitive development of the 20th century. The zone of proximal development was one of his important insights. There are things that a person can do on their own. There are things that are beyond what a person can imagine doing. In between there is the zone of proximal development—what they can learn and what is challenging enough to be motivational. It is by performing in this middle zone where we learn the most and where we are most engaged.

MindShifting: Stop Your Brain from Sabotaging Your Happiness and Success

I've finished" can move a task from any of the other quadrants to the Flow quadrant.

We have discussed how our limbic and prefrontal cortex (PFC) systems operate by default and when they see a threat. We've also discussed how our limbic and PFC systems operate when they are in resourceful and resilient mode, or Sage mode.

MindShifting is about switching our brains from Saboteur mode into Sage mode. Like this.

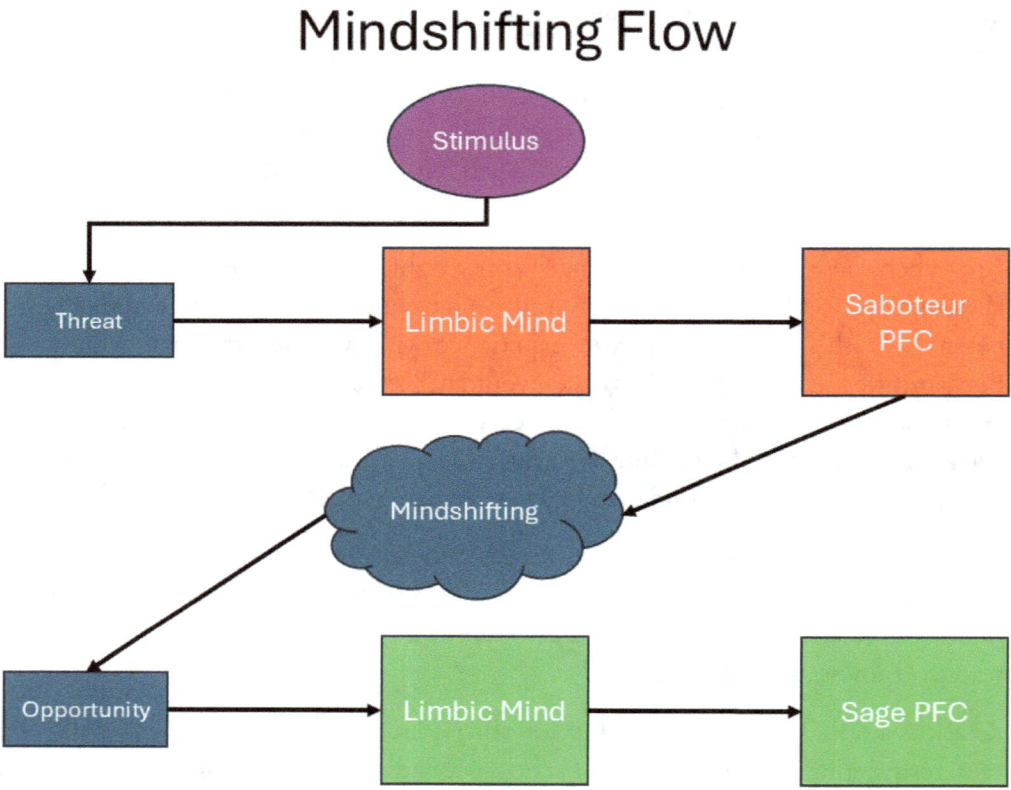

We will now explore the way the limbic brain reacts to a threat, what happens in the Saboteur brain, how MindShifting intervenes, how the limbic brain responds, and then how the Sage prefrontal cortex responds. We will be zooming into each of the four sections of the Full Brain growth mode diagram below.

1. **Limbic Response to Threat:** How the limbic brain responds to an event as a threat
2. **Interceptor and Self-Commander:** How the PFC responds to the threat and how it can be used to intercept and then quiet the limbic reaction

Mastering Our Mind

3. **The Playful Limbic Brain:** How the quieted limbic brain responds to the event as an opportunity
4. **The Resourceful Sage Brain:** How the PFC Sage brain works with an opportunity

Below is a more detailed picture of this model, from threat, to Saboteur brain, to converting the threat into an opportunity, and then to using the Sage brain. We will focus in on each of the sections of this diagram. As complex as this seems, this is a simplified chart of what actually involves tens of millions of neurons in different parts of the brain interacting in a process that is not fully understood.

Full Brain, growth mode

Inspired by Shirzad Chamine, author of *Positive Intelligence*

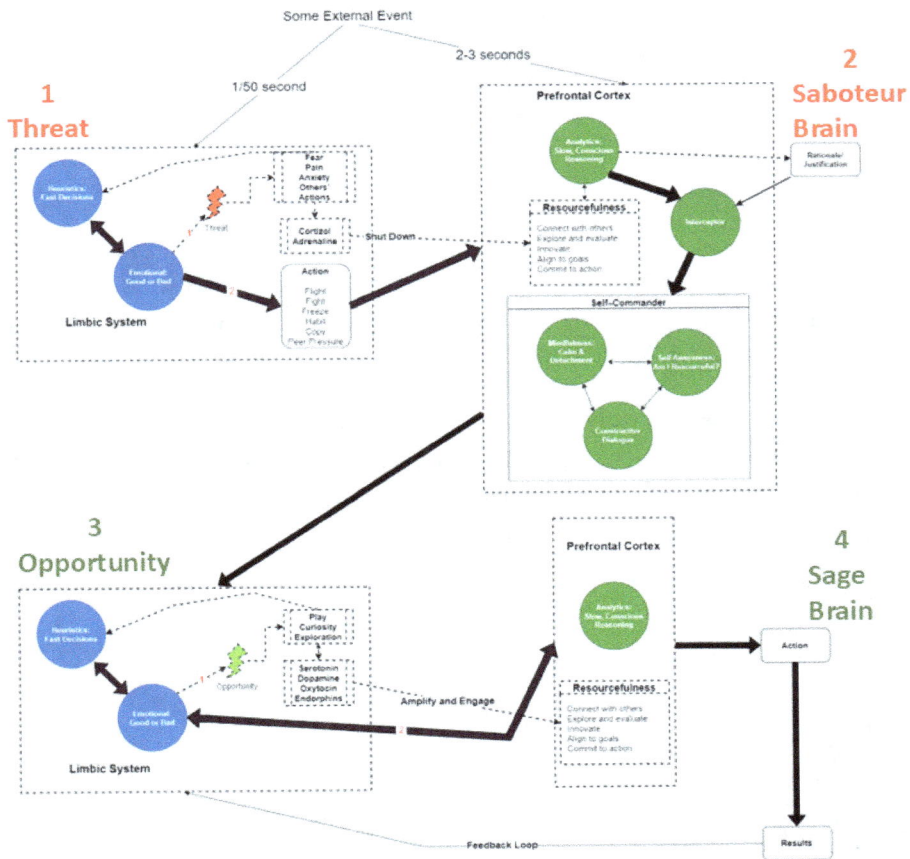

This model is an extension of the work of Shirzad Chamine. He authored a book called *Positive Intelligence*, developed the Positive Intelligence App, and trained a number of coaches to give personal coaching based on his findings.[3]

Chamine coined the term *Saboteurs* for the ways that our brains make decisions from the limbic system. Saboteurs then use stories (which he calls lies) to justify those decisions that inhibit our ability to be resourceful. The Sage brain is what he calls our prefrontal cortex when we are in playful or exploration mode, with five Sage powers.

1. Limbic Response to Threat

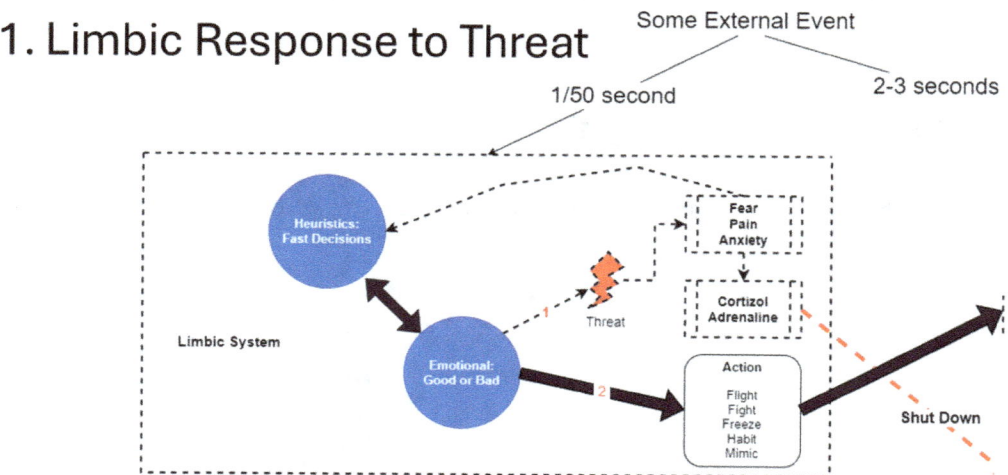

We've seen that the limbic parts of the brain are quickly activated, and often the creative and analytical parts of the brain only come into play after we've come to an action from fear, anxiety, habit, or survival.

What we want to do for ourselves, and what we want to coach our students to do, is to intercept and then change those pathways to decisions and actions that are more productive and effective. I find it tremendously empowering that with training and practice we can be more innovative and effective, and that we can also inspire others to access their own creativity and resourcefulness.

---

[3] Below is a QR code to the Positive Intelligence website:

Our limbic system often senses we are in danger even when we are not in physical danger. It may sense we will become uncomfortable or that we may not succeed at some action or that something is unfamiliar or that someone will get angry with us. Remember the chart with Anxiety, Apathy, Flow, and Boredom. When we don't think we can complete something, we experience anxiety, which then shuts down our ability to perform. When we experience apathy or boredom, we similarly do not engage our Sage minds.

In many cases our brain acts like a Saboteur when anxiety or fear does not correspond to physical danger. Part X and Saboteurs get in the way of our life goals because we are primarily being reactive out of fear, and we fight, flee, freeze, act out of habit, or just go along with what others are doing.

Our prefrontal cortex then justifies that feeling and those actions—our own brain basically lies to us. You can't reason with Saboteurs. When we try to use logic or reasoning, they just dig in and fight back with rationalizations and stories. We can't convince our own Saboteurs to ease up, and we certainly can't convince other people's Saboteurs to let up through logic, facts, or persuasion.

It's easy to see this in others, when they are blaming instead of moving forward, when they are afraid of conflict and so are always accommodating others, when they are playing the victim. With self-awareness we can learn to recognize this in ourselves as well.

Here are seven common ways, and just a small sample from the thousands of ways, that Saboteur behavior is scripted. See if you can recognize these in yourself, people in your family, people you work with, or your students.

- Finding fault or blaming others or ourselves
- Constantly pleasing other people in order to win acceptance
- Controlling every situation and not letting others contribute
- Moving on to greener pastures or constantly multitasking
- Feeling like you are a victim
- Believing that you are not likely to succeed
- Avoiding and procrastinating

My wife has been guilty of all of these.

That's a low shot. I've been guilty of all of these. And so has my wife. And so has every human being on the planet.

All of these cause us, family members, people we work with, students, or others we know to freeze, fight, flee, unthinkingly revert to habits or scripts, or go along with whatever everyone else is doing.

Those are the actions or scripts that we perform.

Once you've looked at those actions, you can also take a look at the stories we tell ourselves to justify those actions. When you, or any of us, say these things, it's generally a sign that you are operating from the survival mind and that one of your Saboteurs is lying to you.

- Egocentrism: Only I can do this, no one else will do a good job.
- Routine: There is only one right answer or one way of doing something. Anything else is wrong, and anyone suggesting that there are other ways or other information is wrong and threatening me.
- Multitasking or task switching: This just came up; let me deal with it and get back later to what I was doing.
- Perfectionism: If this isn't perfect, there will be dire circumstances, so I have to keep doing it. Or it has to be perfect, and I'll never get it perfect, so I should just give up.
- Blame: _____ is at fault so it can't be done. For example, this student never does her homework, this parent is being overly protective, or this person is just trying to cover his butt.
- Procrastination: It can wait until tomorrow.
- Conflict avoidance: Things will be a lot easier if I just ignore this or if I don't deal with it.
- Codependency, or an excessive need to please others: I need to do this so people will like me.
- Victimhood: Bad things always happen to me.

Each of the items on the first list is a Saboteur script we follow, and each of the stories on the second list is a Saboteur lie we tell ourselves and others.

These aren't all-out conscious lies like "The dog ate my homework." The person thinking or saying *these* usually thinks this is "the truth." Remember, as Llinás pointed out, it really doesn't matter to evolution if the brain's model of the world is accurate; if the brain regards something as useful, it's "true."

The stories or scripts above prevent us from being resourceful and so our own brains are lying to us, or as Shirzad Chamine would say, they are examples of our Saboteurs lying to us. Every . . . single . . . time . . . one of these pops into anyone's head, it's a Saboteur or Part X.

Remember, the emotional parts of the limbic system are binary. They judge everything as good or bad, pleasant or painful, opportunity or danger. They are predisposed to look for the bad, because from a survival standpoint, threats might kill us. Being wrong is bad, therefore it is a threat. When someone says we are wrong, that might be a threat, therefore it is bad. Therefore we should fight, flee, freeze, do something quickly from habit, or go along with what everyone else is doing. And if someone says we are wrong, or could do better, or are making a mistake, they are threatening us. Even though in real life, the times we learn are generally the times when we make mistakes or when we are wrong.

Those are indications that we should intercept and reset our brain.

How do you know you are in a script or that you should stop it? With self-awareness or metacognition, we can recognize when we are trapped in the scripts and stories above, which means we should reset.

Once recognized, or intercepted, how do you reset?

2. Interceptor and Self-Commander

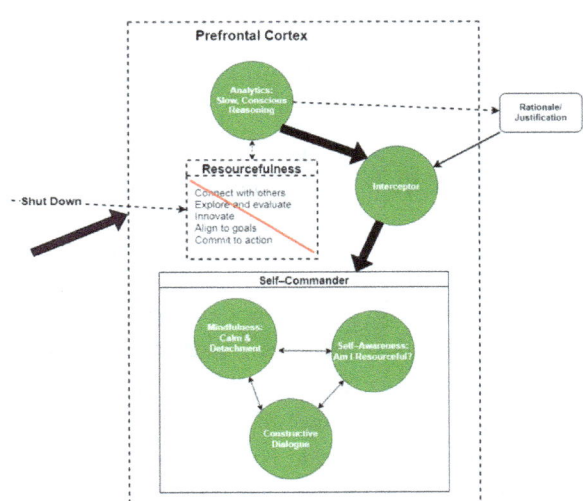

The ability to evaluate one's own reasoning and argumentation, or metacognition, may be the most difficult skill to master.

By default, our prefrontal cortex rationalizes our scripts with these stories, which we interpret as truth.

What we can learn to do, what we can coach others to do, and what they can learn to do is to intercept those rationalizations and then use the Self-Commander to put our brains into opportunity mode.

We *can* use our full brain, as long as we are aware that our first impulse is not necessarily what we should end up doing. We can also help others use their full brains and counter the effects of cortisol and adrenaline.

The first step is to be *aware* that we may be in limbic or survival brain. That's using meta-thinking, and it's a lifetime project. Unfortunately, even if you finish this book and even if you try out all the exercises in this book, your Saboteurs and Part X are still going to hijack your actions and thoughts. Each time we recognize it and defeat them, we strengthen the ability to recognize our Saboteurs. Each time we defeat them, we notch another meaningful victory that we should celebrate.

The first thing we can do is become aware we may be in reaction or lizard or Saboteur mode, perhaps by asking ourselves the questions that we have covered earlier, like

1. Could I be in Saboteur mode?
2. Do I only see one way, or one with a clearly good result and one with a bad result?
3. Do I have to force myself to do this, or will I be doing this with ease and flow?
4. Could I be missing information because of cognitive dissonance or one of the cognitive biases?

The ability to intercept can be improved by preparing for situations that are likely to trigger limbic reactions. A person can be primed to be self-aware of upcoming stressful situations. One teacher told how she had prepared her students in advance to overcome their fear of tests.

> It was finals time, and you can imagine how stressed many students get around finals. A week or so before, I reminded my students that their limbic brains were going to be hyper-active over the next week and were going to tell them to be anxious and afraid. I then asked the students how they could recognize that their Saboteurs were active, and then what they might do to quiet those Saboteurs and return to Sage or resourceful mode. The students and I had a discussion about the limbic and prefrontal cortex modes and how they could transition their brains, and the students asked if they could devote the first three minutes of class to breathing exercises over the next week.

She reported that all the students did great on their finals.

After we go meta, or intercept the limbic or survival or habitual modes, there are three mechanisms for resetting and moving to resourcefulness that we are going to group together and call the Self-Commander: self-awareness, constructive dialog, and mindfulness.

All three can be learned. Not only can they be learned, but with practice, they can become internalized so even they become part of the heuristics that we rapidly deploy.

The first mechanism of the Self-Commander is self-awareness.

In addition to functioning as the interceptor, being *aware* when we are in Saboteur mode may be all that's necessary to quiet the Saboteurs and Part X and change behaviors.

When we become aware, we recognize that we came up with an action or mindset through our primitive mind and that we are defending that action through lies that our Saboteurs are telling us. This gives us the opportunity to look for better alternatives. Metacognition, or self-awareness, is to be aware of the tactics of the limbic or survival brain.

Sometimes this is enough.

Once a person understands the model of lizard brain/thinking brain, limbic system/prefrontal cortex, or Part X/Sage mind and then becomes aware that a story or action is coming from fear, anxiety, or habit, sometimes that person can automatically, without any other action, switch to resourcefulness.

You may be able to do this for yourself, and if you have worked with others, familiarizing them with the limbic/prefrontal cortex model, you might be able to trigger that awareness through a simple question like "Could you [or I] be reacting from your [my] primitive brain, and could there be another interpretation?"

When the limbic mind is directing our thoughts and actions, it's as if we are acting blindly. Here are some other questions we can ask ourselves to shed light on our scripts and stories:

1. Do I see only one choice, or a clearly good and clearly bad choice?
2. Is this what I really want, or am I just reacting?
3. What kinds of emotions do I recognize in myself?
4. What beliefs, values, or actions are mutually contradictory?
5. Are there any threats here, or am I just feeling anxious?
6. What's the best that can happen?
7. Is there a real reason to feel threatened?
8. What kinds of values and needs are related to what I am feeling?

Just think for a second. Do you recognize a time when you have used one or more of these? Can you think of a situation that you face, a friend or family member faces, or a coworker faces where these could be useful?

Remember the example with my dad in the hospital, where he wanted to get out of bed, and I was getting angrier and angrier trying to get him to stay in bed. As soon as it hit me that I was in limbic mode, that realization was pretty much all it took for me to open up.

Anne, a MindShifting class participant, related an incident where she co-regulated a friend (who was already familiar with Saboteurs and Sage mode) using self-awareness. The friend was in fight/flight mode as she felt no one was listening to her. Anne merely asked, "Do you think your Saboteurs might be making you feel this way?" This self-awareness was all it took for the coworker to preserve her sanity. She redirected her attention to something more constructive that she could be doing, which in her case was listening rather than making suggestions.

One of the most memorable times this happened to me was with my son when he was about four years old. We were eating breakfast one morning, and he turned to me and said, "Daddy, I can make you white-hot mad anytime I want." I laughed and continued with breakfast. An hour or so later, we started playing the card game war. Each time we put the cards down, he did the wrong thing. If his card was higher, he'd give the cards to me, and I'd explain that a 10 was higher than a 5 so he won, and I'd hand him the cards. And then if my card was higher he'd take the cards, and I'd explain that a Q was higher than an 8, and I'd take the cards back. No matter how patiently I explained, he would get it wrong every time. It was so frustrating, and I could feel my patience ending.

Then I looked over at him and asked, "Herbie, are you trying to get me white-hot mad?" And he smiled and said, "Mmhmm." And all my anger dissipated. I didn't need to use any of the other tools of the Self-Commander. Just knowing I'd been in a limbic reaction was enough to reset me to playful mode.

Now he's an adult, and his desire and ability to get me white-hot mad has somehow disappeared.

Sometimes just being aware that we might be in Saboteur mode is enough to jolt us back to resourcefulness where we can be creative, critically think, and play with different possibilities. Sometimes we need the other tools in the Self-Commander.

The second tool of the Self-Commander is constructive self-dialog. Most of the examples we covered in the first three chapters were self-dialog techniques:

- Perhaps I can.
- I can take care of this right now.
- Am I in a script or habit?
- What would I love?
- What is the story I am telling myself?
- Challenges help me grow.
- This is eustress.

- Being uneasy or anxious is always the first step to growth; that's exactly how I am supposed to feel when I try something new.
- This is just my limbic brain warning me. Now that I am aware, how can I avoid that danger?
- I can look in my emotional cookie jar at all the difficult situations I've been in where I have succeeded.
- Look at how great I'll feel when I've succeeded (which can be enhanced with the positive anticipation questions).
- I only have to take the next step, then I can reevaluate.
- What would make this more fun?
- What are two more things I can try that might work?
- The first thing one tries rarely works. What can I learn, and what could I try next?

In these cases, first we understood that we might be in limbic mode. Then we used some constructive dialog that opened us up: "Perhaps I can," or "What could make this more fun?" These opened the pathways to our Sage mind, and we could be resilient and resourceful.

The third tool of the Self-Commander is mindfulness.

Mindfulness and meditation are techniques that give us space. They detach the mind from what it was thinking about, worried about, or concerned with. This space can be an effective way to then amplify our ability to use the other two techniques and/or to directly access our Sage and resourceful abilities.

Have you watched world-class athletes? Have you seen them make a mistake, lose a point, fall, drop a ball, or whatever? Watch how they reset. Every one of them uses some mindfulness technique to get their minds to stop dwelling on what went wrong and focus on what they will do next.

The American Psychological Association, or APA, defines mindfulness as "a moment-to-moment awareness of one's experience without judgment." Mindfulness is promoted by practices such as meditation, yoga, and breathing exercises. In fact, many people use the terms *mindfulness* and *meditation* as synonyms.

The APA points out that mindfulness builds self-regulation and executive function practices, and we know how important self-regulation is. They've found that mindfulness brings mental processes under greater voluntary control. When mental processes are under greater voluntary control, this fosters general mental well-being along with development of specific capacities, such as calmness, clarity, and concentration.

The National Institutes of Health (NIH) also notes that mindfulness builds self-regulation.

Many mindfulness practices center on one of the five senses. Here are some ways a person can do quick mindfulness exercises:

- Breath
  - Focus on the feeling in the chest or stomach, sound of breath, temperature of breath, labeling in and out
- Sounds
  - Listen intently to close sounds, far sounds, music
- Touch
  - Notice the sensation of feet on the floor, of sitting, of touching and rubbing an object, of rubbing two fingers together
- Sight
  - Observe colors, shades, textures, or the shape of a common object
- Another person
  - Focus on details like voice tone, cadence, eye color, skin tone, hair, or clothing
- Walking
  - Focus your mind while walking to what you see or hear around you, especially in nature

In the practice of mindfulness, we reset our minds by focusing on sensations and by dismissing other intruding thoughts. When we are controlled by our limbic reactions, our conscious mind keeps up a dialog to continue to focus our thoughts on what is troubling us. Mindfulness doesn't combat those thoughts, it replaces them with calmness, and as we get better at using mindfulness to reset our minds, we get better at gently pushing those thoughts away.

There are tons of books and apps for mindfulness. I use two apps regularly:

1. **Insight Timer**, which has thousands of free mindfulness tracks on all different topics and timeframes, plus premium content, and
2. **Equa**, which was created by the Health and Human Performance Laboratory at Carnegie Mellon University and focuses on using mindfulness to promote equanimity.

A sample mindfulness exercise might be to focus on breathing:[4]

1. Take one or two deep breaths.
2. Now, listen to your breath as you breathe in and breathe out. Notice the sound as you breathe in. Now notice the sound as you breathe out. Notice the difference in the sounds. Breathe in, breathe out. Listen. Listen again as you breathe in and breathe out.
3. Now we will change to a different sensation of breath. Feel your chest or stomach expand as you breathe in and contract as you breathe out. Notice how it feels as it expands when you breathe in. Notice out it feels as you breathe out. Feel yourself expand as you breathe in. Feel yourself contract as you breathe out. Do this a few more times. In, expand. Out, contract. In, feel the expansion. Out, feel the contraction.
4. Now, notice the temperature of the air as you breathe in and then as you breathe out. Think about the temperature of the air you breathe in. Think about the temperature sensation of that air as you breathe out. Notice the temperature as you breathe in. Now as you breathe out. Do this a few more times, paying attention to the temperature of the air.
5. Now we will be conscious of the act of breathing in and out. As you breathe in, say to yourself "in," and as you breathe out, say to yourself "out." As you breathe in, say "in," and as you breathe out, say "out." Do this a few more times.

And another sample might be to focus on touch or feeling:[5]

1. Rub two fingers together.

---

[4] You can practice this breath mindfulness exercise by listening here:

[5] You can practice this kinesthetic mindfulness exercise by listening here:

2. Take the fingers of one hand and move them from the tips of the fingers of the other hand down your palm and then back up.
3. Feel the way your feet rest on the floor.
4. Feel each of your toes. Wiggle your toes.
5. Clench or tighten one of your calves, and then relax it. Then the other calf, and then both calves.
6. Feel where your hands or arms are resting. Notice each spot where they are touching something else. Imagine all the sensations as you focus on what you feel from the tips of your fingers, up your arm, and then back down.

When I first started mindfulness practices, I might get 30 or 45 seconds into it and my brain would remember a past argument, or some problem I'd been working on would demand attention. Sometimes, I'd follow those thoughts and give up on the mindfulness. Other times, I'd start getting upset at myself for failing mindfulness. Either way, the Saboteur mind would win.

Everyone who practices mindfulness has thoughts come up during their exercises. We all learn how to gently push them to the background. The ability to consciously direct our attention is a foundation of well-being.

When a distracting thought occurs, we learn to say things like "not now" or "let me do one thing at a time and go back to my breath" (or my focus on touch or my focus on my hand, or whatever you are focusing on during the mindfulness). For me, once I become aware that some other thought is hijacking my mind, my breathing becomes my anchor. I calmly say to myself, "I can return to that later," and then I pay attention to some aspect of my breath—how my chest expands and contracts, the temperature of the air in my nose as I inhale and then as I exhale, or some other aspect of breathing.

I find that when I do finish the mindfulness practice, I can focus on the problem or situation with a clear and resourceful mind.

There are two ways to use mindfulness. The first is to do some mindfulness practice every day. I generally do 10–15 minutes of mindfulness practice every morning after I wake up. There is research that shows that if we do mindfulness in the morning each day, we fuel our minds to be resourceful throughout the day, and we will tend to rebound more quickly.

The other time to do mindfulness is in the moment. When we are frustrated, anxious, angry, etc., if we can take 30 seconds to five minutes, we can often reset our minds.

Here are two examples of using mindfulness to reset the survival mind.

Example 1:

> Mary offered Samantha, a friend of hers, some furniture she wasn't using because the friend was moving with her children away from a toxic relationship. When she and Nancy, another friend, went to deliver the furniture, they found that Samantha was completely frazzled about leaving and moving, had not packed, had no plan, and was clueless. Mary and Nancy could see all the plans they had made for the rest of the day evaporate. They were going to be stuck for the entire day organizing, boxing, carrying, and transporting because Samantha was too disorganized and clueless to have prepared for the day. They had their own families, their own kids, their own plans. And all that was going out the window because of Samantha. They could feel the anger bubbling up. Any of us would have.
>
> Mary intercepted those feelings. She and Nancy did 15 minutes of breathing mindfulness exercises. They then asked themselves what was most important to them, and what was most important was to make sure their friend and her kids were in a safe place and set up to go on with their lives. One of the highest types of joys a person can have is to be of genuine help to someone they care about. The move became a joyful experience. What a great turnaround, right?

Example 2:

> Teresa recounted how her brain was telling her that no one would ever consider her qualified for a good job because her experience wasn't relevant. Nobody was going to listen to her. She didn't even have a valid certification.
>
> She realized that there was a Saboteur party going on in her brain. That was the interceptor. She did a mindfulness exercise for about 12 minutes and felt some relief. She went through all the ways she had conquered difficult challenges before, as in being the only woman in a 100-person engineering firm, rising through the electrical worker ranks despite the odds being stacked against her. And she came up with a few next steps she could take that were doable in the short term and would give her more confidence. And when her Saboteurs raised their ugly voices, she responded with the riddle, "How do you eat an elephant? Little by little."

Our Saboteurs and survival brain are smart and tricky. On the list at left below are some of the lies that they tell us that lead us to make choices that are suboptimal.

Countering the Survival Brain

Only I can do this, no one else will do a good job

_____ is the only way to do this, I have no choice

Multitasking or task switching (let me do this, too—squirrel)

This has to be perfect

Blame (____ is at fault so it can't be done)

It can wait until tomorrow

I won't deal with this so I can avoid conflict

If I don't do this, no one will like me

Bad things always happen to me, so I might as well just stop

Interceptor

Self-Commander, accessing your resourcefulness:

1. Self-awareness
2. Constructive dialog
3. Mindfulness (10 seconds or more)

⬇

Feelings of play, curiosity, and exploration

Once the Saboteurs activate, our brains release cortisol and/or adrenaline, which inhibit our resourcefulness.

We can intercept those stories and scripts with our self-awareness interceptor.

We can then disengage from the fear and anxiety hormones by activating our self-awareness, constructive dialog, or mindfulness, or some combination of the three. Only after intercepting and then self-commanding are we able to reactivate based on a feeling of play, curiosity, and exploration.

Resetting the brain means that we can start acting out of opportunity rather than fear and anxiety. This is the crux of the SCORE technique from chapter 3, becoming aware that we are in limbic mode, reenacting what it feels like to be in Sage mode, anchoring those Sage feelings, and then trying them out in the previously stressful situation.

3. The Playful Limbic

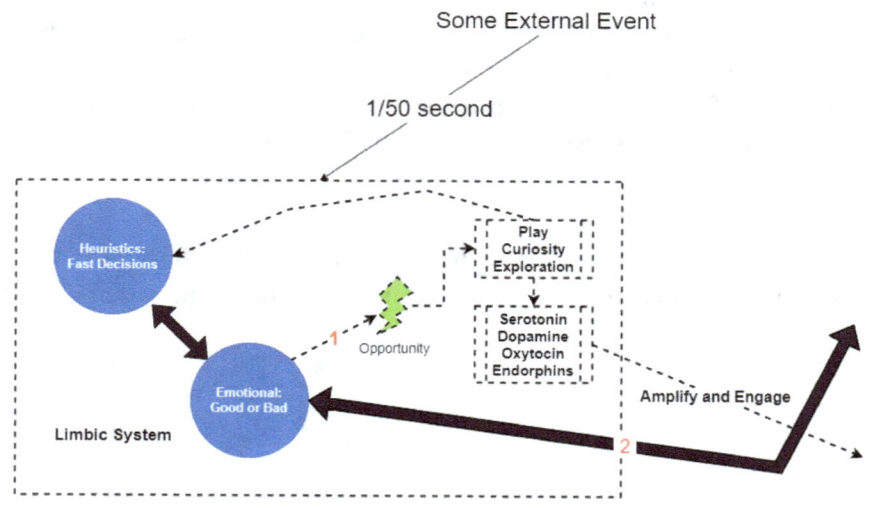

Without fear, we can approach situations with a sense of play, curiosity, and exploration. This triggers the joyful hormones of serotonin, dopamine, oxytocin, and endorphins, which all amplify and engage our prefrontal cortex or Sage mind.

When we use our Sage mind, we are essentially working through situations by

- empathizing and really listening to others, and empathizing with ourselves as well,
- exploring relevant information and evaluating that information with curiosity rather than judgment,
- synthesizing new plans and building on what others are suggesting,
- evaluating and aligning actions based on higher-level goals, and
- enthusiastically embarking on actions even when we know that we may need to make adjustments as unforeseen obstacles temporarily block us.

4. The Resourceful Brain

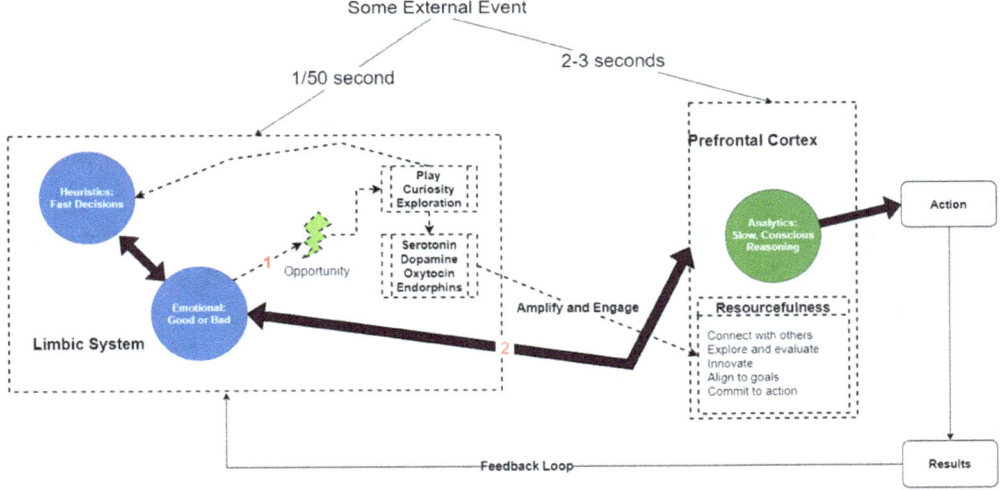

The resourceful brain is playful and curious, using what Shirzad Chamine calls our five Sage powers: empathy, exploration, innovation, navigation, and focused action.

This is when we experience flow, when we experience challenges as eustress, when we enjoy learning because we are in Vygotsky's zone of proximal development.

Chapter 4 Review

If you think back to the beginning of this chapter, our default way of thinking is fight, flight, freeze, habits, or mimicking. These often result in actions that contradict what we say and think our values and goals are, which is a form of cognitive dissonance. If we or someone else challenges our actions or thoughts, our limbic brains perceive a threat, we disregard the data (confirmation bias), and we resist, releasing cortisol and adrenaline, which means:

1. We are focused on defeating or avoiding whatever is threatening us.
2. We revert to a story that rationalizes what we have already decided, and we double down on that story being the truth.
3. The resourcefulness of our prefrontal cortex gets shut down, which means we are not able to empathize, explore, innovate, align to goals, or commit to action with ease and flow.
4. We fall prey to cognitive biases such as confirmation bias and are unable to use new information or feedback to reconsider our position.

Human beings cannot get out of limbic or survival mode by logic or data. Once we are in limbic mode, we can only become resourceful by first realizing that we are in limbic mode, which is a type of metacognition we have called intercepting, and then using one or more of the three methods of the Self-Commander to quiet our limbic emotions and reactions and then tap into our resourceful prefrontal cortex.

Because human beings are wired to stay in unthinking limbic mode once we enter it, we are primed to fall victim to people who are skilled at putting us there. Advertisers and marketers use this to convince us that everyone else is happy and using their products. Politicians and media use this to convince us that we are in some grave danger, and once we react with anxiety and fear, we are much more likely to follow their directives, and not only follow them but also disregard any information that shows they are wrong and fight against anyone who disagrees.

Those who can interrupt their limbic reactions and then self-command themselves to a resourceful state can wrestle back command of their own thoughts, and the manipulators will have lost their power.

Let's return to Sandra from the beginning of this chapter. She often felt anxious and overwhelmed by too many responsibilities. She turned that around when she realized that her internal dialog around being too busy or too tired were her Saboteurs lying to her to "protect" her. What did she do?

She did a 10-minute mindfulness practice to clear her mind. With a clear mind, she decided that the next time she heard herself saying she was too busy or she had no time, she would say to herself, "Imagine how great you are going to feel when you do it anyhow," and she would do it at that moment. She also decided that if by any chance that did not work, she would frame that incident as having been a chance to practice or a chance to learn, and she would just come up with something else to try next time.

But it worked. She got more accomplished, and she really was a lot happier.

When she came up with her actions and also how she would react with ease and flow even if she did not achieve the result she wanted, she was using the Sage innovate power and the Sage perspective.

In the next chapter, we will explore how those five powers of the Sage mind and the Sage perspective help us to be more effective and happier.

CHAPTER 5

Unleashing Our Own Brilliance

Karine teaches middle school. Here is how she used her Sage powers.

There is this one girl. She sometimes doesn't come into the class. She rarely completes or hands in her homework. She's quite smart but loves to make the rules. No matter what I did, I couldn't reach her, and her actions and lack of response were triggering stories about her being a "bad" kid, not trying, not worth the effort to help.

I decided to model the exploration and empathy Sage powers.

I went and sat next to her in the hall at the high-top counter she often sits at during class time. I watched her watch reels for a minute, then asked about what kind of reels she likes most. She said cooking. I explored that response. It took me by surprise, and I guess my comment that I like watching cooking shows surprised her as well.

She shared with me a bit of the dynamics at home. Her family was sick, and she was in charge of cooking dinner. She wanted to make sure it was healthy, full of veggies. She shared she has a little sister she takes care of. No mom, just dad and grandparents. She had assumed the "mom" role in the household: cooking, cleaning, etc.

I was able to make some connections. I asked what it was like to be the "mom" at home and then come to school and be treated as a child, and whether that was why she didn't do what teachers told her to do.

When I expressed this to her, she looked at me with glossy eyes and nodded yes. I had such empathy for her in that moment.

She told me she's super smart and can do a lot of the stuff we ask her to do.

I told her I knew that. And the reason I harass her to try is because I see the potential in her and want her to show it off: get the grades, earn the diploma, land a good job, and be a successful human.

I feel we are going to make real progress this year. What a difference, having a conversation as a curious individual rather than through judgment.

When we are acting in Sage mode, we are in an emotional state of play, curiosity, and exploration. Our happiness is to a certain extent the result of our brain releasing the happy hormones of serotonin, dopamine, oxytocin, and endorphins.

Model of the Sage Mind

The above model of the Sage mind shows five powers we all possess when we are in Sage:

1. Empathy, connecting with others
2. Exploring and evaluating
3. Innovating
4. Navigating, setting and aligning to goals
5. Focused action, not just to act, but with a commitment to overcome anticipated and unanticipated obstacles, even though we don't fully know how we are going to succeed

When our minds are using any of these powers, we generally have a feeling of happiness and concentration, which Mihaly Csikszentmihalyi called flow. Being in Sage is less about what we are *doing* and more about how we are *feeling* about the situation we are working with.

When my wife asks, "Would you like to take out the garbage?" (which I've learned is not actually a question but an imperative), taking out the garbage is almost always the correct thing to do. My action of taking out the garbage could be from Sage, or it could be a limbic reaction. If my reaction is "Why is she bothering me with this?" or any one of a number of negative stories, I am in limbic mode. If my reaction is "Yes, I would like to contribute my share and take out the garbage," or any one of the many positive emotional reactions, then I am in Sage mode.

Either in limbic or Sage mode, I take out the garbage. In limbic mode, I am sullen and resentful, while in Sage mode I am happy and engaged.

When we are in our survival or limbic mind, we do not have access to the five powers or the feeling of happy engagement. Our energy is directed toward moving away from whatever we are feeling. When we have learned to intercept our limbic emotions and then use our Self-Commander to quiet our anxiety, fear, or negative reactions, we can feel playful and curious and have access to our Sage powers. It is much less important which of these five powers we are using than that we are in Sage mindset. Often, just a conscious decision that selects any one of the Sage powers and then a resolve to use it can switch us to Sage mode.

What is it like to use the Sage powers? How can we consciously choose to utilize these powers to be more effective and happier? Here is a fuller exploration of each of these powers.

Empathy

Compassion for yourself

Compassion for others

Seek to understand, walk in their shoes

Ask from curiosity, not judgment

Imagine:
    This person is locked in Saboteur mode
    How can I connect limbic to limbic

Image generated by Google Gemini

Empathy is all about connecting to and having compassion for the person. The opposite of empathy is judgment or blame.

Empathy is relatively easy when everything is going well. It's harder when you are angry, arguing, or having a difficult time.

Of course, even when things are going well, we can still react from survivor or Saboteur mind:

- Someone succeeds: we are jealous
- We succeed: we think we did not deserve it
- Somebody has good luck: we feel their success is not deserved, and maybe let them know that
- Someone compliments us: we feel we do not deserve the compliment, and perhaps let the person know why the compliment isn't really warranted

Here are some examples of things going well, with empathetic responses:

- Someone succeeds: you are genuinely happy for them and express it
- You succeed: you feel good about what you accomplished
- Somebody has good luck: you are happy for them
- Someone compliments us: we are happy to receive the compliment

When things are going well and we share the praise, when we compliment a person, or when we let someone know we are happy for them or proud of them, we are showing empathy.

When things start to go wrong, our limbic system will judge or blame in one of three ways:

- We can blame ourselves
  - "You are such an idiot . . ."
- We can blame others
  - "They screwed up . . ."
  - "This person is so demanding . . ."
- We can blame circumstances
  - "If the traffic wasn't so bad . . ."
  - "If the internet wasn't so slow . . ."
  - "I'm just doing what everyone else is . . ."

These are all limbic reactions, and we've learned that we cannot tap into any of our Sage powers when in limbic or survival mode.

Sometimes we can rapidly switch from blame or judgment to empathy, just like when Karine was originally judging her student and then told herself to try empathy.

Maybe when we feel we are starting to blame, we can consciously choose to use the empathy power. Sometimes we need more than intercepting and self-talk.

Maybe we will first do a mindfulness exercise. When the limbic dialog is quieted, we can actively affirm, "I'm going to use my empathy power to be resourceful."

We can prime ourselves to be empathetic. When we are about to have a difficult conversation, we can take a moment to prepare ourselves to ask and listen with the purpose of connecting. We can prepare ourselves so that when we feel ourselves starting to judge or feel upset, we can tell ourselves it's just our Saboteurs, and we can stay in empathy and connection.

Just as you sometimes blame and chastise yourself, and sometimes you judge, blame, and chastise others, you can also empathize with yourself, and you can empathize with others.[1]

Empathy for ourselves

We all beat ourselves up when things don't go right. "You're an idiot." "How could you mess up so badly?" "You don't deserve to be successful." We all say those things about ourselves.

Empathy for self means finding a way to still respect and honor yourself even when things do not work out the way you had hoped. Even when you "know" it's your own fault—that's just a story; you can still give yourself grace.

Here are some examples of positive self-talk statements we can make that show empathy for self:

- Wasn't that funny!
- Let's learn from this.
- Everyone makes mistakes. I can forgive myself and move on.
- I am going to celebrate the effort I put in and then see what I should do next.
- I am not defined by my failures. I am defined by how I respond to them.

My mom was one of the best at this of anyone I've ever known. Something would go wrong, maybe due to something she did. She'd say "Whoops!" and then she'd

---

[1] This is the essence of the SCORE method from chapter 3, using an anchor to trigger a Sage response.

kind of giggle. And then it would be over, and she'd go on to whatever needed to happen next.

One of the most memorable times this happened was when we were helping my dad at work one weekend in July. He ran a computer service that often printed out lengthy reports for manufacturers and importers. One of his clients needed to send monthly statements to their thousands of customers. We ran the program, printed the statements, and then needed to run the computer printout through a burster, cutter, and folder, which would separate the statements, cut them to size, fold them, and stuff them in the correct envelopes.

The temperature felt like it was over 100 degrees, and the building air conditioning did not operate on weekends.

My mom brought over an industrial fan, turned it on, and whoosh, thousands of sheets of papers blew all over the room. The entire job needed to be rerun.

My dad was furious.

My mom could have reacted in any one of a number of different ways. She could have blamed herself. She could have yelled back. She could have cried.

But she looked around. She let out a "Whoops!" She started giggling, and she said, "Look, it's snowing in July."

Soon we were all laughing.

We started the job running again on the computer, went out for a meal, came back, and finished the job without further incident and in a great mood.

Choosing to be happy can be a great tonic.

What do the best athletes do when they make a mistake? They forgive themselves and move on. Later, they use that mistake to learn. They reset their minds (through some mindfulness), embrace who they are, and focus on what's next, not what just happened. You can watch Roger Federer talk about this at minute 13 of his 2024 Commencement Address at Dartmouth (scan QR code below). What you are doing is the most important thing you are doing while you are doing it. And once it is over, it's over. Period. Maybe it can be useful as feedback to make you better or stronger.

Can you use empathy toward yourself when you look at past failures rather than acting as a victim or parceling out blame?

Here is how one person described using self-empathy:

> I recently got a grant to build an outdoor classroom at our school, and we had a tight timeline to take action and start spending the funds. I'd been feeling a lot of self-doubt about moving the project forward and feeling out of my depth in decision-making.
>
> I intercepted that and directed empathy to myself: I don't have to be perfect, I don't have to do this alone, and I was the one who won the grant so I couldn't be completely incompetent.
>
> I pulled together a committee from the school along with admin, and together we charted our path forward. It helped me be open to learning from the expertise of others and brought to the forefront all the things we needed to consider and how we could proceed.

Empathy for others

Empathy for self doesn't mean deflecting blame to someone else. Blaming others is still Saboteur behavior and doesn't lead to Sage resourcefulness.

I had a boss who had a way of deflecting blame from himself, but it would still be blame; his words and actions would still be out of anxiety, fear, or anger. He would construct a story to exempt himself when things went wrong, but he'd often find a way to blame someone or the situation. We've all had bosses and family members do that. That's not empathy.

Burned into my memory is a time when I worked for him as a salesperson. I was about 25 years old, and I had a really good prospect. Our standard rate for the particular service this prospect needed was $4,500 per month, and I went to my boss and told him that I could close it at $4,000 a month. He said that good salesmen don't discount and that he would come with me and show me how to close business. The two of us made the call, and during the call the prospect talked about their business and how their costs were up and their profits were down, how our system could help them, but that he was worried about the costs, and my boss proposed that we would charge them $3,500 a month, which the client accepted, and we left with the contract.

After we were out, I said, "I told you that I would close him at $4,000 a month, and you told me good salespeople don't discount. And then you closed him at

$3,500 a month. What gives?" And his response, which I now recognize was a story generated through his limbic mind, was, "The difference is that you were just giving him a reduced cost, but I found out what he needed and charged him a rate we could both live with. You would have blown the sale."

Yes, he gave himself a break, but exonerating yourself while putting another person down is not empathy.

Sage mode is being curious and playful. As the employee on the butt end, I felt he was being defensive and emotional.

A playful, curious person will seek to understand, without judgment, the experience and perspective of others, getting the others to talk about what they believe, value, experience, and know with the purpose of understanding, not arguing.

What my boss did, not just to me but as a way of acting, was he judged. He did not seek to understand the experience and perspective of the other person.

Empathy is to experience what it's like in someone's shoes, to understand the experience and perspective of others.

A boss with empathy might have been curious about the situation. That boss might have drawn out the salesperson's thought process:

- What made them think that the prospect wanted to purchase the service?
- Why did they think that the prospect was not going to purchase it at full price?
- What had they done or said to justify the full price?
- What made them think that the prospect would buy at that reduced price?
- What if the prospect did not buy at that price? What would they do, and what would they learn?
- What could they try to still close at full price?

If you are seeking to understand someone from the perspective of changing them or improving them, that's not empathy, that's control. Seeking to understand from empathy is seeking to understand because you are curious and want to strengthen the connection.

When I disagree with another person or when I feel another person made or is making a mistake, and I talk to the person with the purpose of changing them, my limbic feeling is, "I just want to tell this person to do X."

I have to intercept that and use my Self-Commander to connect to my empathy power. I find I have to redirect the limbic self-dialog to "No, I just want to find out what this person really wants or needs or feels and how they feel this action will get them there. That will be a way to connect with them, and once we are connected, we can collaborate to work out what to do."

Once you have a connection, you and the other person can find common ground and most likely avenues to pursue that common ground. Without the connection, you are not using your empathy power.

Here is how one MindShifting participant described the process of empathy:

> It can be very difficult at times to empathize with my middle school kiddo at home because of how emotional and irrational he can become. Many of his problems seem so small to me that it's easy to overlook how big of an emotional response they can evoke from him. I declared this week that I would tap into my empathy power when we interacted.
>
> It's been very eye-opening being more mindful and empathetic of his feelings so I can respond to him more appropriately.

Sometimes you approach another person with a suggestion or to offer support, and even if you feel empathy, their Saboteur reaction is to be aggressive, to attack. You make a move to connect and WHAM, the person you are trying to connect to or influence makes some statement or takes some action that must have been calculated to piss you off.

Using the empathy power, you're building connection, cooperation, and collaboration, *even in the face of aggression, conflict, and opposition.*

It's hard to stay in Sage mode trying to build empathy when you're being attacked. The MindShifting: Conflict and Collaboration class spends over six hours on different techniques to resolve these types of situations, but here are two possible techniques to maintain your resilience and empathy:

1. **Game**: Can you make a game out of who can last longer, *you* as a curious person trying to connect or *them* as an aggressor trying to make a win/lose interaction?
2. **Trapped Victim**: Imagine that this person (which could be yourself) is someone who is blocked by their Saboteurs. Inside there is someone who is joyful and innocent, but this person is trapped by Saboteurs who are stoking fear, anger, and anxiety. How could you really connect with the inner person and thereby enable their positive thoughts and emotions? How could you convert stress into eustress?

Empathy does not mean giving in.

You can have empathy and still have rules. Let's say you are a parent, it's 30 degrees outside, and your child wants to go outside without a coat. Empathy does not mean having a discussion until you reach a mutually acceptable outcome. Empathy might mean letting them know that you understand their wish, that your role is to keep them safe, and sometimes that means you have to set and enforce rules that they are not going to like. This is one of those times. They have every right to feel upset or angry—in fact, you probably would be upset as well if you were in their shoes. You and they are both good people. And if they are going to go outside, they have to wear a coat.

You can be firm *and* sympathetic.

Empathy promotes a caring culture where people appreciate each other as human beings and feel safe to be authentic and vulnerable. Empathy does not mean you are in agreement with what a person is doing or saying. It's putting yourself in a position to experience their perspective. The path to influence and persuasion generally leads through empathy.

Exploration

No blame or judgement

Curiosity and sense of wonder

Fascinated anthropologist or researcher
- What is happening
- What took place
- What actions are being considered

The second Sage power is exploration.

When I think of exploration, one of the images I see is a child walking along the shoreline, turning over rocks just to see what's under them. That child is probably asking themselves, "What else can I find out? What's over there? Wow, what's that?"

We can be like that child once our Sage brains, our curiosity and our sense of play, are activated.

Let's say my wife and I disagree about what we should do next weekend, and I say, "Let us explore why I am right."

No, that's not the Sage explore power. That statement is Saboteur mentality—it's judging and arguing, not Sage exploration.

Explore mode is exploring just for the joy of exploring. There is no blame. There is no judgment. Exploration is beginner's mindset:

- being open to new ideas
- asking questions to understand
- questioning assumptions (yours and theirs)
- embracing differences
- actively listening
- being curious
- embracing mistakes and setbacks as opportunities for learning and growth

While exploring, we are not planning how we can get information that bolsters what we already think we should do. We are not exploring for the purpose of bolstering what we already know or believe.

Shirzad Chamine suggests that you explore by imagining you are a **fascinated anthropologist**. An anthropologist examines what makes us human. They study what people do, how they interact, what they produce. A fascinated anthropologist might be trying to understand what makes us different and what makes us the same.

As a fascinated anthropologist, if my wife's idea of what to do this weekend differed from mine, we would have a conversation to find out

- what she wanted to do,
- how she felt we both would find enjoyment,
- what my motivations were, and
- how she felt about those.

I would participate in that conversation from a point of curiosity to learn about her motivations and what was influencing the decision. And I would be curious about her reactions to my suggestions. This is a conversation, not an inquisition. Over the long- and short-term, these types of conversations result in stronger relationships.

We often look at how other families act and interact and judge them. We can contrast the way a fascinated anthropologist versus a judgmental person would go about evaluating how a family interacts in a different culture. The judgmental person would likely have preconceived notions and stereotypes about the culture. They would likely highlight differences in actions as flaws and make snap judgments about what the family is doing right or doing wrong. They would be likely to try and impose their views and values on the family.

The anthropologist using the explore power would strive to understand the family's interactions within the context of their own culture. They would invest time in building trust and rapport with the family and immerse themselves in the daily life of the family to gain a deep understanding. They would show respect for the family's beliefs and practices, trying to understand rather than impose.

As a fascinated anthropologist, you are trying to piece together how people act and adapt in different situations, what the situations are, how they come to understand the situations, and what they do.

I saw many examples over the years as a volunteer working with US families that were hosting international teenage students for the school year.

What happens when an American parent talks to their Pakistani exchange student and the student is looking away? Isn't that a sign of disrespect not to look at the person who is talking to you? That's a judgment.

In the dominant culture in the US, you look directly at another person when they are talking to you. In many cultures in Asia and Latin America, a young person never looks directly into the face of an elder. For them, looking away is showing respect.

What happens when a US worker asks their coworker in India to perform some task, the person from India agrees, and then the task is not done? And what happens when that happens repetitively? Is that Indian worker lazy? Dishonest? Those are judgments.

What if a fascinated anthropologist found out that in Indian culture, the appropriate response to any question is to respond with what the other person wants, and there are other nonverbal cues to what the result will be? That's a way Indians stay connected and avoid contentious confrontations. By exploring, a fascinated anthropologist would use their curiosity to find that there is a communications gap between the US and Indian workers. It's not one side being lazy and the other being obnoxious. Each side just needs to find out more about the other's expectations and ways of communicating.

AFS, the high school international student exchange program, uses the statement "It's not right, it's not wrong, it's just different" as a tenet of training students and host families who are about to get immersed in another culture, prodding them to explore instead of judge.

Using the explore power, you're looking at causes and possible outcomes, not to blame, not to achieve specific results, but just for the knowledge: possibly to connect better with that other person because you are curious and engaged. Later, after you have accumulated the knowledge, perhaps that knowledge becomes usable, but that is not the driver for asking questions and exploring.

Let's say I am cooking on the stove and do not turn the exhaust fan on. The house gets smokey, and the fire alarm goes off.

My wife might say, "What happened?" If she is asking the question out of anger or so that she can then use whatever my answer is to yell at me, she is not asking that question in explore mode.

If she is merely curious and is going to accept the answer with no judgment, then she is in Sage explorer mode.

In fact, she is more likely to influence my future behavior if her questions resemble the fascinated anthropologist than the disappointed spouse. Being in Sage and using exploration is consciously not making anyone wrong. One of the reasons we've stayed married for 40 years is that we both know that.

The phrases "What happened?" and "Help me understand" can be Sage or they can be judgmental.

It's not the phrase that determines if you are using the Sage explore power. It's your state of mind. The emotions of exploration are curiosity and wonder—curiosity and wonder without blame and judgment, just figuring out what is going on. Most of us telegraph our mindset, so if we are asking those questions judgmentally, we are most likely going to encounter resistance.

Imagine being a teacher, and a student did not hand in their homework. "Why didn't you hand in your homework?" might be our question. Asking it judgmentally would be with the attitude that the student is wrong and needs to be corrected. And that judgment may, in fact, be correct. While judgment and then the next action are limbic responses, that does not make them wrong; it only makes them instinctual. To be in explorer mode, you might

1. Look at what you did in class before assigning the work, not from the point of view of blaming yourself but just with a sense of curiosity.
2. Explore what the student did with their time instead of doing their homework, not from the point of telling the student what they should have done but from curiosity.
3. Examine the student's attitude about homework, not from the point of blaming them or their parents or even yourself, just from curiosity to see if this offers any explanations.

Karine and all the other teachers at her school had no effect on her student's behavior using judgmental questions and controlling statements.

Controlling a situation is a limbic response. Exploring might be considered the opposite of controlling.

Imagine someone is doing something, and you are afraid that they will not do it on time, or maybe you are anxious that they will not do it satisfactorily and the results will be bad for them and possibly you.

If you act from that fear, perhaps by following up to make sure they are progressing or by letting them know where they are not doing a good enough job, then you are in limbic or survival mode.

This does not mean that you have to accept shoddy work.

If you act from a sense of exploration, you might be curious about whether they can have the time, skills, and/or motivation to handle the work. Through mutual exploration, perhaps you can generate ways for the two of you to make this fun and also get the task done well and on time. Perhaps the discussion can be eustressful.

In each of these situations, if you engage from a feeling of fear, if you act from limbic mode, you cannot access any of the Sage powers; you must be in Sage mode to access Sage powers. From survivor mind, you need to intercept the Saboteurs, use your Self-Commander to get into Sage mode, and then you can tap your explore power.

Explore does not mean that you need to ignore downsides, risks, or consequences.

Jane McGonigal, in her book *Imaginable: How to See the Future Coming and Feel Ready for Anything—Even Things That Seem Impossible Today* recommends using a balanced approach to exploration.

> **Positive imagination** asks the question: What's something good that could happen? It builds confidence that the future will be better. **Shadow imagination** asks the question: What's something bad that could happen? It builds readiness to face future challenges. Whatever your instinctive feelings are about the future right now, you will benefit from cultivating at least a little bit of the flip-side feeling.

True exploration means curiosity about positive and negative outcomes. Said with a feeling of curiosity, each of the following is a powerful Sage exploration question:

- What could go wrong?
- What is the worst that could happen?
- What if it's not done on time?
- What if they beat us?
- What if we mess up?

Can you use the explore mode to look at past failures or to look at some situation that isn't going well or that is frightening rather than judging yourself or others?

Exploration and empathy often work together, so the information you find out by knowing the back story can also build empathy. Look at the similarities: no blame or judgment, curiosity, and a sense of wonder.

Exploration and Empathy

No blame or judgment

Curiosity and sense of wonder

Fascinated anthropologist or researcher
- What is happening
- What took place
- What actions are being considered

Questioning from curiosity often creates connection

Knowing the back story can build empathy

When you use empathy, you are blamelessly exploring the emotions, situation, stories, and goals of the person you are empathizing with. When you use exploration, you will also be exploring the emotions, situation, stories, and goals of that person, in essence empathizing with that person.

Exploration and empathy lead to collaborative problem-solving processes such as **mutual learning**. Mutual learning requires curiosity and a willingness to listen. It is a powerful set of techniques to avoid and resolve conflicts and is based on four key values to an interaction:

1. **Valid information**: you resolve and signal that you will reveal all relevant information you have on a subject, whether it supports your position or not.
2. **Free informed choice**: no party is coercing any other party toward a particular path. You seek to create an environment for people to agree to do things because the information flow is transparent, not because they feel manipulated or coerced.
3. **Internal commitment to the decision**: once a decision is made, people commit themselves to do whatever is necessary to implement it, and they hold themselves and each other accountable.

4. **Compassion**: you, and as the process proceeds, all involved, temporarily suspend judgment in order to understand other people's perspectives from a mindset of curiosity and letting go of judgmental reactions.

Here is a contrast between a conventional conversation and one using mutual learning. In this case, you and a coworker are working on a project, and the project needs the coworker to finish the report they are working on tomorrow.

In the conventional conversation, "you" are trying to convince the coworker to complete the task. Note how judgment is embedded in the conversation. You are judging that the coworker is holding up the project; they are judging that you are pressing them.

Conventional Conversation

You: Hey, I really need you to finish the report by tomorrow. It's crucial for our project timeline.

Coworker: I'm sorry, but I have other tasks that are high priority. I can't get it done for another five days.

You: I understand you have other tasks, but this report is really important. Can't you prioritize it just this once?

Coworker: I really can't. My schedule is packed, and I have deadlines for other projects that I need to meet first.

You: But if you don't do it, our whole project could be delayed. Can't you just push your other tasks a bit?

Coworker: I wish I could, but I'm already stretched thin. I'll try my best, but five days is the soonest I can manage.

You: This is really frustrating. We need this done now, not in five days. I don't see why you can't make it a priority.

Coworker: I'm doing the best I can. I really can't change my schedule right now.

You: Fine, but this is going to cause problems for the project. I hope you understand that.

In the mutual learning conversation, you approach the conversation with a sense of curiosity. Note how empathy and exploration are used to share valid information, free informed choice, generate internal commitment, and share compassion.

Mutual Learning Conversation

You: Hey, I noticed that our timeline calls for the report to be completed by tomorrow. Can we talk about how we can manage this?

Coworker: Sure. I'm really swamped with other tasks right now. I don't think I can get to it until five days from now.

You: I understand you have other priorities. Can you share a bit more about what's on your plate?

Coworker: I've got a couple of deadlines for other projects, meetings, and some urgent client requests that I need to handle.

You: It sounds like you're juggling a lot. The report is also critical for our project. What can we do to make sure both your tasks and the report are managed effectively?

Coworker: I'm not sure. I really can't push back my other deadlines.

You: What if I help with some of your other responsibilities? That might free up some time for you to work on the report.

Coworker: That could work. If you could handle the client requests and maybe one of the meetings, I might be able to delay one or two other priorities and fit the report in.

You: I can definitely take on the client requests and attend the meeting for you. Does that give you enough time to work on the report?

Coworker: Yes, that would help a lot. I could then finish the report by tomorrow.

You: Great! Let's keep each other updated on our progress. I appreciate your flexibility on this.

Coworker: Thanks for your understanding and support. I'll make sure to get the report done.

You: No problem. Let's do this together.

Using the exploration and empathy powers is a powerful way to defuse potentially confrontational issues. It starts with attitude: no blame or judgment, curiosity, and a sense of wonder.

There are clear guardrails: commitments to (1) honestly share vital information, (2) avoid trying to control, (3) arrive at a mutually agreed decision, and (4) communicate with compassion.

MindShifting: Stop Your Brain from Sabotaging Your Happiness and Success

A great question to get into explore/empathy mode is, "If I were using my explorer powers with empathy, what information would I want to learn, and how would I ask the question?"

Innovation

Collaborating to devise and select solutions
1. Yes, and
2. What can we try first
3. Imagine the other side is 10% right
4. Imagine you are 20% wrong
5. What I like about that

The third Sage power is innovation.

Robert Dilts described Walt Disney's rubric for innovation in his book *Tools for Dreamers*:

- **Dreamer**: New ideas emerge in dreamer mode. What is it we want? What are possible solutions? Anything goes, nothing is filtered out.
- **Realist**: Practical solutions are explored in realist mode. What is achievable and when? How can we use the ideas of the dreamer to make this happen? What is the action plan?
- **Critic**: Troubleshooting happens in critic mode. What could go wrong? What is missing? What are the weaknesses?

These are three discrete modes of creation. In life, too often we go directly to realist or critic mode: I know what the problem is. This is what we should do. This is why *your* idea won't work.

The innovation Sage power requires all three modes: staying in curious, playful dreamer mode longer than most of us feel comfortable, transitioning to realist with the purpose of coming up with one or more actions that we think will work, and then using critic mode to prepare us to avoid or overcome obstacles.

When you are anxious, just proceeding from habit, or certain that you know what to do, you are not in a frame to be innovative. Declaring that you are going to tap into your innovative powers in relation to a task or strategy places you on a different course and opens up the possibilities of your own mind.

We each possess an ability to innovate on our own. This is **individual innovation**. We also have the ability to collaborate and take advantage of the different experiences and viewpoints of others, to tap into diversity. This is **group innovation**.

While being an innovative individual is a strength, it can also be an obstacle when taken too far. One trap we all fall into is coming up with an idea and then feeling the need to convince others it is the best one.

If you "*own*" an innovation, if you control the conversation toward "*your*" solution, you lose out on the power of the group. As Angela Maiers says, "The smartest person in the room is the room."[2]

Group innovation means collaborating to devise and set up solutions. Group innovation begins with curiosity, a genuine interest in different opinions and in others. A good metaphor is when people in a group innovation setting think of themselves as earthworms.[3] Earthworms process and aerate the soil, making fertile ground of the nutrients of sunlight, water, and detritus to nurture the next cycle of life.

Earthworm-innovators provide space for everyone to participate, making the ground fertile for the beginnings of new ideas and diverse viewpoints and experiences, to nurture the process of generating robust solutions. Earthworms don't claim credit for the plants that grow.

I'm sure we all can recall many instances where we are working with others and we start noticing that we, and probably everyone else, is spending as much time shooting down what everyone else is saying as we are spending moving toward a solution.

We do this society-wise as well, issue after issue. This is our limbic brain taking charge.

The limbic brain operates from our assumptions and heuristics. The Sage innovate power escapes from those limitations, and, as with all Sage powers, first requires one to be in Sage mode: to be curious and playful instead of judgmental or fearful.

Here are typical examples of giving an appearance of innovating but succumbing to the survival mind:

---

[2] Angela Maiers first said this in her 2014 Ted talk. The internet seems to give credit to David Weinberger from 2015. Angela is a friend of mine, and I'm going to give the credit to her.

[3] The earthworm metaphor came via Adrienne Maree Brown, in her book *Emergent Strategy*, and she credits Jenny Lee of Allied Media Projects as the originator.

- In a meeting to discuss the launch of a new initiative, one member brings up an idea of using augmented reality, and the leader responds, "We've already tried that, and it didn't work. Let's stick with tried-and-true methods. Does anyone else have any ideas?"
- A group is tasked with a project, but the project hits an obstacle. One of the members shoots down new ideas with "We just need to work harder and everyone do what they said they would."
- Teachers are getting together to discuss improving student achievement in science, perhaps using new technology. A few of the teachers dominate with "We've always used textbooks, and they have always worked fine."
- A couple are discussing what to do during the weekend, and one says, "We can do anything you want as long as it doesn't interfere with my golf games on Saturday or Sunday." The other, feeling resentful, responds, "Why do you always . . ."

The survivor mind jumps to critic, and not from the vantage point of preparing to meet obstacles. The survivor mind uses criticism for the purpose of stopping change. It's an extension of Part X, the "invisible force that wants to preserve the status quo, to keep you from growing or changing, that blocks your evolution and potential."

Earthworm-innovators who are participating in a group innovation make the ground fertile for new ideas and diverse viewpoints. They stay in dreamer mode until everyone feels heard—listening, asking questions, and clarifying. They are aerating and not judging or passing judgment. Similar to the other Sage powers, the innovate power stems from a feeling of curiosity and play.

If you go into meetings or discussions thinking there is only one right answer, you are probably not going to innovate with a group of people.

If you go into meetings or discussions with the frame of mind that no one really knows what is going to work but that some actions will evolve as a result of brainstorming and discussion, then you are in the right frame of mind to be an earthworm-innovator. Part of innovation is to work with as diverse a group as you can to come up with many different perspectives and alternatives to try that might move you in the general direction of where you want to go.

The goal behind innovation practice is to work with others to build something that is better than if any one of you came up with a solution on your own. Contrast the situations below with the earlier ones:

- In a meeting to discuss the launch of a new initiative, one of the participants brings up the possibility of using augmented reality. The next person

responds, "What I like about that is that that technology is very exciting, and what we could also do is come up with incentives for people to adopt the initiative." That process of "what I like about that is . . . and what we could also do is . . ." continues until each person has felt they have been heard.
- A group is tasked with a project, but the project hits an obstacle. One of the members offers that everyone just needs to work harder. The next person says that is one suggestion and asks for some other things that they could try as well. The group focuses on a few small steps that they could experiment with and monitor the results of, then they can get back together to discuss and figure out next steps.
- Teachers are getting together to discuss improving student achievement in science, perhaps using new technology. One person brings up that the existing textbooks have been fine. Instead of arguing the point, the next person responds, "Exactly, we need to take what's working from the textbooks, and what else can we do?"
- A couple are discussing what to do during the weekend. One suggests going to a location where they can take hikes. The other says they are fine with anything as long as it doesn't interfere with their golf games on Saturday and Sunday. The first then offers, "Maybe going away for hiking was wrong, and you need your golf to relax. Perhaps we can come up with some options that we can do together, like a day trip to the beach. What other possibilities could we do?"

Here are the techniques used in those examples that spurred group innovation:

1. **Yes, and:** Instead of explaining why someone's idea is wrong (yes, but), insist that each person start out with what they like about the idea and then share what other thoughts they have.
2. **Probes instead of solutions:** Perhaps think of little steps rather than a grand solution—"Let's try this and this and regroup so we can assess."
3. **Finding agreement:** Imagine that the other side is 10 percent right. Where might they be right? Can you force yourself, especially when you think you are right and another person is wrong, to really look for how they might be 10 percent right, and then express what is right about what they are proposing or saying?
4. **Admitting imperfection:** Imagine that your side is 20 percent wrong. Where might you be wrong, and where might others help you? People often let down their defenses when you admit that you are wrong about something. Can you critically look at whatever you have been saying or

proposing to find the 20 percent of what you are saying that is wrong, and then articulate that and credit the others?

These are techniques to move your mind to be able to pursue and accept different actions and possibly results. When your brain is in this mode, you are in sync with resourcefulness, and you can better align groups with resourcefulness.

How do you envision using the innovation powers of the Sage mind?

Navigation

Success is feeling grounded and anchored
1. What is really important
2. If I were in total sage mode, what would I want
3. What would I love
4. Is this the 80% or the 20%
5. If I were at the end of my life looking back, what would be important
6. What would my wiser elder self say
7. What would someone 100 years from now want me to have done

The fourth Sage power is navigation. Navigation is about choosing from different paths based on deeply held values or what gives life meaning and purpose.

Navigation is being explicit about what is truly important and not getting lost in the weeds. It's keeping our eyes on the final destination. When you feel you are aligning your actions or tactics with what is really important, you feel grounded and anchored, even if what you are proposing to do is difficult or risky.

My wife and I went on a five-day bicycle trip in Uruguay once. At the tour operator's where we picked up our bicycles, I asked the tour booker for a map or directions, and her response was, "Here are the five towns you will be staying in and the addresses of the inns. Just keep riding with the ocean on your right and you'll find all the destinations." Unfortunately, Uruguay did not allow US-based phones to use the phone network. But understanding what was important, keeping the ocean on our right, allowed us to find our way. Yes, we put on some "bonus" miles at times, but as long as we kept the ocean to our right, we never got too lost, and we could always recover.

Navigation is like that, just keep in mind what your priorities are, or your highest goals, and don't be too attached to any one strategy. Understand that sometimes it won't look like you are making progress, but the actions and the results will fall into place, and the little things just won't matter.

Here are some situations contrasting reacting to a situation and making decisions using navigation.

- A person receives a job offer at a high salary.
    - Reflexively, the person either accepts that new job or rejects it.
    - Using navigation, the person considers their passions, long-term goals, and effect on family, and they follow the path that they think would lead to greater fulfillment and motivation.
- A community faces an issue.
    - Reflexively, local authorities get quickly in gear and implement quick-fix solutions, which leaves certain community members feeling left out and disadvantaged, resulting in the community being divided and some residents facing ongoing hardship.
    - Using navigation, authorities do triage where necessary and engage with community members to understand needs and values, then develop a longer-term plan that takes into account housing, mental and health support, transportation, education, and access to jobs. The community understands the trade-offs and becomes stronger and more resilient.
- A person with less experience than you describes what they are going to do next, and you know that they will not succeed.
    - Reflexively, you either correct them or do it yourself, and the task gets done.
    - Using navigation, you reflect that this particular task is less important than them learning how to think through projects on their own. With that in mind, and knowing how they operate, you come up with a way of letting them learn from their mistakes while also not endangering themselves or others.
- You are expecting someone to meet you at a certain place and time. As usual, they arrive 20 minutes late with a bunch of excuses.
    - Reflexively, you get upset and chastise them.
    - Using navigation, you realize that the two of you have 45 minutes together, and what would be really nice is to enjoy that time. You decide to focus on making that time pleasant and engaging, and that before you meet with them next time, you will have a plan B for them arriving late that you will communicate to them empathetically.

The last example is applying the **pareto principle**, which can be a good foundation for the navigate power. The pareto principle states that 80 percent of what happens to us has little or no long-term significance, and that the remaining 20 percent makes 80 percent of the difference in our lives.

If 80 percent of the things we instinctively get upset at make up only 20 percent of the difference in our lives, wouldn't it make sense to focus our efforts on the 20 percent that account for 80 percent of the difference?

Let's say you are at a restaurant and your food comes overcooked. You might get upset. Using navigate, you might ask yourself, Is my food being overcooked tonight in the 20 percent of the things that affect my life, or is it in the 80 percent that I can just let go of? If it's in the 80 percent, you can focus on what's really important, maybe the conversation you're having with others at the table, or maybe you can just bring it to the restaurant's attention, being curious about what they then do. You're not going to waste a lot of time, effort, or emotion on it. But if having an overcooked meal that night at that restaurant is in the 20 percent that's really important, you are going to expend the energy to make things right.

I faced a dilemma with my dad where the Sage power of navigation was particularly helpful. At the time he was 96 years old with moderately severe dementia. I was with him two days a week, and he would continuously complain about things that were wrong: nobody was visiting him, his computer wasn't working, his wallet was missing, I hadn't been there for two months. Arguing or showing him he was wrong would sometimes work, but 15 minutes later, he would start up again as if we hadn't just discussed it. It was very frustrating and brought out fight/flight reactions in both of us.

Where navigation helped is when I went deep within and asked myself what was really important. The answer that came back was that the most important thing was that he was comfortable and had moments of joy as often as possible for whatever time he had left on earth. With his comfort and happiness as the prime motivators, interactions became much more enjoyable. My first response became to ask myself, "What would give him greatest joy now?"

"My wallet is missing" prompted "What would give him greatest joy now?"

"You haven't been here for two months" would again prompt "What response would give him greatest joy now?"

It didn't really matter if the answer made me "wrong." He'd forget in a few minutes anyhow. But his emotional well-being, and my own happiness at seeing him happy, were what really mattered.

On the other hand, if my wife is wrong, she's just wrong.[4]

Here are some of the questions you can ask yourself to prompt being in navigation:

- What is really important?
- If I were in Sage mode, what would I want?
- What would I love?
- Is this in the 80 percent or the 20 percent?
- If I were at the end of my life looking back, what would be important right now?[5]
- What would my wiser elder self, myself in 20 years, advise me to do at this point?
- What would someone 100 years from now, in the real long term, want me to have done in this instance?

The Sage navigate power keeps us focused on what is important and lets us let go of what is not.

Focused Action

What are you going to do

How will you react when something doesn't go right

How will you react when your Part X tries to stop you

Maintain a feeling of ease and flow

Curiosity and play instead of fear and anxiety

The fifth Sage power is focused action. Focused action is being in ease and flow, enjoying acting even when there are obstacles or setbacks.

You are already familiar with being "in the zone," or being in flow. Visualize how a Jedi Knight would be totally present knowing that they will be effective by quieting

---

[4] That is meant as humorous sarcasm. If my wife and I disagree, she's probably at least 10 percent right.

[5] If someone is late for a meeting, is this something that you're going to look back on from your death bed and count as an important moment in your life? That kind of puts things in perspective, doesn't it?

and centering their mind. Visualize Roger Federer in his prime losing a point. What does he do to stay in Sage and get ready for the next point?

That's the feeling we want with focused action, and often that comes from being prepared so that our Saboteurs cannot deflect us. Because they are going to try.

Nothing goes perfectly well all the time.

Part X or the Saboteurs are going to throw all their weight behind disrupting the Sage mind whenever bad stuff happens. They will trigger fear, stress, anxiety, guilt, urgency, shame, disappointment, hate, and victimhood, attempting to shut down the prefrontal cortex and put limbic reactions front and center.

Metacognition (Chamine's the Interrupter) and equanimity (the Self-Commander) are the two weapons that can defeat them. The 12 self-talk methods covered in chapters 2 and 3 can be powerful shields.

The people we are interacting with are also likely to use those same triggers to put us into Saboteur mode, and we can use the same internal weapons to avoid their traps.

Let's say there is a person who always finds a way to upset you. Maybe they put down your ideas. Maybe they always one-up you. Maybe they criticize everything you do while maintaining that they are perfect or always right or at least always better than you. I have encountered many people who've done that to me at many different stages of my life.

I have learned to imagine being in focused action while being in a conversation with these people. My focused action might be, "I am going to stay calm and resourceful, and whatever they say, I'm not going to fly off the handle. I'm just going to stay calm, maintain a sense of humor, and remain in Sage."

Maybe I use the Robert Dilts SCORE method from chapter 3 and set up an anchor to bring me back to Sage when I feel myself slipping.

When I feel anger or anxiety rising, I can do a 15-second mindfulness practice, like feeling my breathing or focusing my gaze on something. If we are at a point where I am supposed to say something, I can say something like "Go on," "Tell me more," or even "Can you explain that again?" to keep them going while I am resetting.

If that doesn't reset me, I can come armed with some phrases to postpone action, such as, "I'll need time to process. Let's come back to this [in a half hour? Tomorrow?]." Even if they insist that this be resolved right away, I can be secure in just saying, "I feel I need until [whenever], and we can resume then." Being firm does not mean being angry. One can be politely firm about setting boundaries or limits.

Unleashing Our Own Brilliance

The other side might become angry, but that is their limbic reaction and their problem.

Another technique I have used to foster focused action when confronting an annoying situation or person is to make the encounter into a game, to see how long I can maintain Sage mode, to see if I can maintain Sage mode for the whole meeting, or to see which one of us persists longer, them trying to upset me or me staying calm and resourceful.

This can also be very helpful dealing with "customer service" from a typical healthcare insurer, airline, cable company, bank, government agency, or large company. The game is how long you can feel in Sage despite their efforts to have you get off the call without them making any effort to resolve your issue.

Remember, it's not their lack of helping that is causing your anger. Their responses are just the situation. Your emotions are your reaction. Your reaction can be under your control with a resolve to stay in Sage.

My sister Sue has always been the best at this in our family. She remains in control, and she also remains on the phone, asking more questions with curiosity, making more suggestions without being attached to the other person agreeing. She could stay on the phone doing this for hours. Sometimes she makes no more progress than we do, but she also gets results a lot more often than the rest of us do. And she does that by remaining engaged with ease and flow, with curiosity rather than frustration.

Focused action in whatever one is doing means staying in Sage, maintaining a sense of what Csikszentmihalyi called flow, despite obstacles and despite the efforts of our Saboteur mind to react to those obstacles with fear or anxiety or a sense of giving up.

Feeling fearless is pretty similar to the way people feel when playing a video game. They try something. It doesn't work. Game over. They try again. Obstacles don't bother them; that's part of the excitement. They try something, their character dies, and they have learned that something doesn't work, so they can now try something else.

My mom always said, "Chance favors the prepared mind." When we arm ourselves to overcome our Saboteurs, we can better maintain our feeling of focused action. Perhaps you might ask yourself:

- What might I tell myself when my Part X or Saboteur mind tells me to quit, and how will I overcome that?
- What are a few things that could go wrong, and how might I handle them? (Doesn't that sound like a healthy critic in the Disney innovation model?)

- I know there will be times I will feel anxious, that's part of trying something new, so how will I stay in Sage?

When we are in limbic mode, our brains have secreted cortisol and/or adrenaline to focus our minds but also to inhibit our prefrontal cortex from resourcefulness.

We can intercept that and use one or more of the three Self-Commander options to transform to Sage mode: self-awareness, constructive dialog, and mindfulness.

Once in Sage mode, we have the five Sage powers available to us. A Sage **intention** is a choice to deliberately deploy one of the Sage powers:

1. I am going into this situation using the Sage power of **empathy**. My goal in interacting with others is to connect with them just for the purpose of connecting.
2. I am going into this situation using the Sage power of **exploration**. My goal is to just explore different possibilities. I will ask questions without any preconceived judgments to find out more because I am curious about where they will lead.
3. I am going into this situation using the Sage power of **innovation**. My goal is to open up new possibilities (even better if I can open up new possibilities in a group setting) and ask questions about how they might work, and I will look for the positive in all possible actions raised.
4. I am going into this situation using the Sage power of **navigation**. My goal is to find the higher values of all parties and work together to find ways to meet those values rather than merely choose some specific actions.
5. I am going into this situation using the Sage power of **focused action**. My goal is to anticipate what might keep us from achieving our goal and the ways we will overcome those obstacles.

One of the most fun exercises I've done is to declare a Sage intention or focus for a day. If I choose empathy, I'll say, "Today, each time I interact with someone, I will use my empathy power. I will try to find out what they are thinking and try to put myself in their shoes."

When you declare a Sage intention of any one of these five powers, it puts your mind in gear to be resourceful. It doesn't really matter that much which of the five powers you choose; don't spend a lot of time thinking about which is the best or the best for you. Just pick one and see if you can be that power for the rest of the day, and then reflect on what that was like. You're going to find that the act of choosing unleashes your capabilities and the feeling of flow.

Here is one person's observation from declaring a Sage focus for the day:

> I declared "empathize" and "navigate" as my Sage powers for the day. I found that when the people I interact with feel that I understand their points of view and they understand how my questions and suggestions are aiding them in reaching their goals, they are more open to dialog and changing directions.

And here is a parent's observation:

> Leaving the house in the morning has lately been chaos. We've had a lot of nights where the boys' bedtime has been pushed way back, and so no one gets up and going on time, and then as we try to leave for school it devolves quickly . . . and I've been noticing that I contribute to that by completely losing it, and that is so counterproductive and not the mom nor the example I want to be for them.
>
> So last night I decided to declare "navigate." I asked myself, "Is this what I really want, or am I just reacting?" And the answer came back, "No!"
>
> Just knowing that allowed me to make a plan.
>
> Just knowing that I had a plan made me much more self-aware. Honestly, I thought we were going to make it through the morning with ease. But of course we had a bathroom emergency as we were trying to get in the car, as the other was wandering around still not putting his shoes on. I totally felt myself click into limbic.
>
> And again I used navigation to ask, "What do I really want?" This very much helped me to pause, take a breath, and recognize this was not that big of a deal. Now if only I can be prepped for every adversity. 😊

Declaring a particular Sage power can have the effect of encouraging an environment of play and curiosity, which engenders resourcefulness.

I dare you to try it for a day before reading the next chapter.

Chapter 5 Review

When we are in Sage mode, we are curious, joyful, creative, and persistent. We are in flow.

Being in flow gives us access to five powers: empathy, exploration, innovation, navigation, and focused action.

In your life, you have experienced each of these powers. You have the ability to tap into any or all of those powers. When you feel challenged, you can appeal to any of the powers; they are all part of you.

You can also help others tap into their own Sage powers. Each of the five statements above can be reworded:

1. What if you go into this situation using the Sage power of **empathy**; what if your goal in interacting with others is to connect with them just for the purpose of connecting?
2. What if you go into this situation using the Sage power of **exploration**; what if your objective is to just explore different possibilities? How would you ask questions without any preconceived judgments to find out more, just because you are curious about where they will lead?
3. What if you go into this situation using the Sage power of **innovation**; what if your goal is to open up new possibilities and ask questions about how they might work? How could you look for the positive in all possible actions raised and build on them rather than shoot them down?
4. What if you go into this situation using the Sage power of **navigation**; what if your goal is to find the higher values of all parties and work together to find ways to meet those values rather than merely choose some specific actions?
5. What if you go into this situation using the Sage power of **focused action**; what if your goal is to anticipate what might keep everyone from achieving the goals, and then to find ways to overcome those obstacles?

Imagine the impact you can have by unleashing these powers in yourself and in others!

CHAPTER 6

The Realist's Guide to Happiness

On Saturday evening, Maureen and her husband discovered a water leak in their second bathroom. Her reaction to situations like this was normally classic limbic. She would think, "Why do things like this always happen to me?" She would get angry that someone had done something and not fixed it. She would feel anxious that this would take a long time to fix and be very expensive, and that this was a sign of a lot of other problems with the house, and she would be fearful that her husband wouldn't respect her because he knew more about pipes and plumbing than she did.

This was a classic Saboteur party going on in her head, resulting in her freezing from taking constructive action and lashing out at her husband.

In this chapter, we will talk about the tools that she used to handle the situation with resilience.

In the previous chapter, we explored the five powers of the Sage mind, which are the source of human resourcefulness and resilience.

They only operate when our limbic mind is in a relaxed mode. The fear-based or anxiety-based survivor mode inhibits the Sage powers, and so we need to intercept what our brain is doing and then use the Self-Commander to quiet our Saboteurs and Part X so that we can be resilient and resourceful.

Mindfulness is a very strong tool to reset the brain. Even if we are extremely upset, angry, or fearful, when we take 15 minutes, or even less, to devote our attention to the here and now, we can restore our ability to be resourceful, curious, and playful. We quiet the limbic fear hormones and start secreting serotonin, dopamine, oxytocin, and endorphins. Those hormones amplify and engage our Sage minds to use the five Sage powers.

No one is capable of blocking out all distractions during mindfulness. Whenever we are concerned with some issue or event, our minds dwell on that. Those concerns will try to interrupt our mindfulness practice. In performing mindfulness, whenever we sense our minds drifting to whatever is troubling us, we can gently come back to the mindfulness exercise, and that gives us the space to reset our limbic system and tap into our Sage brain.

When the brain is reset, we effectively remove the elements of fear and anxiety. This allows our survival mind to release its hold that controls our prefrontal cortex and allows us to actively engage that part of our brains. We experience a sense of play, curiosity, and exploration. It is when we are playful, curious, and exploratory that we experience Sage mode, and we know our prefrontal cortex is engaged.

Here is a quick summary of the five Sage powers.

Empathize	Visualize the person as someone who is being terrorized by Saboteurs, and your mission is to find out how they feel and what they need. Sometimes we are upset at ourselves, but if we've used the Self-Commander to reset, we can empathize with ourselves as easily as empathizing with someone else.
Explore	Be curious about what has happened and what will happen without being attached to any results. Sometimes people will say something and we will be dismissive; when we are playful, we genuinely want to find out more about it without judging it.
Innovate	Encourage and build on others' ideas to create something new when the obvious or traditional ways aren't working. The innovate power is not primarily about *us* being innovative, it's about us *working with others* and feeding off each other to come up with possible actions that are better or different from what any of us could have designed individually.
Navigate	Using a consistent internal compass, what are your priorities? What would your wiser older self say? You might ask yourself what is important and what you really want to accomplish, or if some point is something you'd care about in 10 years, and if not, then focus any solutions on what really is important.

Activate	Be prepared to be in flow, especially when obstacles appear and your Saboteurs or Part X start playing with your motivation. You know that the first thing you try is unlikely to completely succeed, and you are prepared for obstacles and opposition from your Saboteurs and from others. Focused action means embarking on action prepared and excited to overcome whatever surprises pop up, even when we don't fully know how we are going to succeed.

When we sense that we are reacting using our limbic or survival brain and not being resourceful, we first intercept, then use the Self-Commander, then activate the Sage mind with a sense of playfulness and curiosity, and then maintain that Sage mind even when we start feeling stress or we sense we are drifting back to limbic mode in the face of distractions or obstacles.

Toward Resourcefulness and Resilience

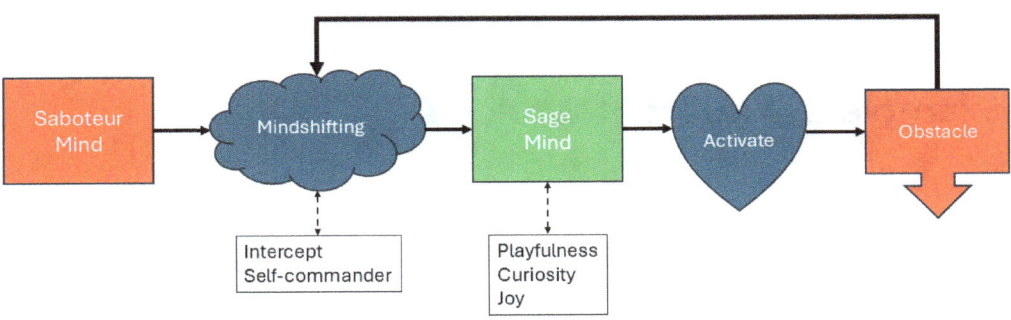

Here are three examples of how that process might play out.

Example 1: Public Speaking

Scenario: Alex has to give a presentation in front of a large audience but feels extremely nervous.

1. **Intercept Thinking:** Alex notices their thoughts spiraling into worst-case scenarios like forgetting lines or the audience reacting negatively.
2. **Quiet Limbic Reactions:** Alex takes deep breaths, grounds themself by feeling their feet on the floor, and focuses on calming their racing heart.
3. **Approach with Curiosity and Playfulness:** Instead of dreading the presentation, Alex decides to treat it as an experiment to see how they can

connect with the audience and how their story might resonate. Alex imagines how it will look and feel to connect with members of the audience; how they will smile and nod their heads when they agree and the look of concentration as they listen. Alex takes a moment to imagine the feeling of finishing the talk on a high note, the exuberance of success, and the excitement of having overcome obstacles. During the talk, Alex will look for smiles and positive headshakes as feedback to confirm their connection.

4. **Stay in Flow:** Even though thoughts crop up about people not liking the presentation, Alex maintains focus on the audience's reactions and adjusts the tone and pace based on feedback, ignoring distracting thoughts about possible mistakes.
5. **Sense of Joy:** Despite initial nerves, Alex feels engaged with the audience and experiences a sense of accomplishment once the presentation is over.

After quieting our limbic reactions, we have the opportunity to choose how we respond in Sage. This is a good example of the positive anticipation method described in chapter 3.

Example 2: Conflict at Work

Scenario: Jamie has a disagreement with a coworker over the direction of a project.

1. **Intercept Thinking:** Jamie catches themself thinking their coworker is being unreasonable and that the project is doomed.
2. **Quiet Limbic Reactions:** Jamie takes a moment to step back, perhaps by taking a short walk, to reduce feelings of frustration and anger.
3. **Approach with Curiosity and Playfulness:** Jamie decides to understand their coworker's perspective better using exploration and empathy, which makes the disagreement an opportunity to explore new ideas, which triggers the innovate power.
4. **Stay in Flow:** Jamie listens actively during the discussion, asking questions to clarify their coworker's viewpoint. When the coworker voices disagreement, Jamie asks qualifying questions to uncover higher-level goals, indicating what they are learning, adding to suggestions instead of arguing with them, and looking for common ground rather than focusing on conflict.
5. **Sense of Joy:** Jamie and their coworker collaboratively find a new approach that integrates both viewpoints. Even after the meeting, disagreements surface and tempers flare, but Jamie and the coworker are able to reset back to their common goals and values, leading to a beneficial project outcome.

Many of us, even after quieting our limbic reaction, would focus on "not getting angry." As we learned in chapters 2 and 3, a strategy of *stopping* feelings or actions does not work. In this case, Jamie chose to *replace* their feelings of anger and impatience with the playful Sage powers of exploration and empathy.

Example 3: Exam Stress

Scenario: Casey's parents have made it clear that Casey is expected to maintain an A average. Casey is afraid that they might not perform well on the final. They keep on replaying the anticipated conversation after the parents show their disappointment because Casey froze and received a C on the final exam.

1. **Intercept Thinking**: Casey recognizes they are catastrophizing, imagining failing the exam and its consequences on their future.
2. **Quiet Limbic Reactions**: Casey uses mindfulness techniques, such as focusing on their breath and doing a brief meditation to calm their mind.
3. **Approach with Curiosity and Playfulness**: Casey reframes studying as a chance to test their knowledge and see how much they've learned, treating the exam as a challenge rather than a threat. They draw on their emotional cookie jar by remembering that they have often been anxious about tests and have generally performed well.
4. **Stay in Flow**: During study sessions, Casey remains focused on the material, using short mindfulness activities and positive self-talk whenever they sense that they are being sidetracked by failure.
5. **Sense of Joy**: Casey feels more confident and engaged with the material, and the exam becomes a manageable challenge rather than a source of fear.

Note that Casey did not tell themself to stop being afraid or not to be anxious. They chose to use focused action. They knew that there were going to be times before the exam when they would start feeling stressed, and they primed themself to use mindfulness and positive self-talk to return to Sage.

In these examples, one thing that remains clear is that MindShifting is not a one-and-done act. Whatever we do, internal Saboteurs and outside obstacles are always going to pull us back to survival mind.

In addition to the five Sage powers, Shirzad Chamine also introduces something he calls the **Sage perspective** and what Phil Stutz calls **radical acceptance**. The Sage perspective is a great way to reset after obstacles or undesired outcomes.

The Sage perspective, or Stutz's radical acceptance, is about treating things that go wrong as potential gifts or opportunities. Our minds often catastrophize things that did or might go wrong. The Sage perspective allows us to accept negative or unforeseen events or outcomes and move on or even use them as motivators.

If we think about it, most of the things we get upset about aren't going to make any difference to our lives in the long run. Remember the pareto rule, that says that only 20 percent of the things that affect us make 80 percent of the difference, which also means that 80 percent of the things that affect us really don't make much of a difference. If we can let go of the unimportant, we can ensure that the important gets done.

With the limbic mind, we feel anxiety or fear or anger. We start blaming ourselves or the situation or others.

Let's say I'm about to teach a new lesson, and I'm afraid it won't go well. Maybe I'm gripped by anxiety and thinking of just skipping it. One aspect of the Sage perspective is similar to the navigate power. I could just ask myself, If it doesn't go well, in five years will I care that on this day a lesson didn't go well?

Whether what we are doing is in the important 20 percent or the less important 80 percent, we can also ask ourselves, How is this a long-term gift? There are three types of gifts:

1. **Gift of learning**: What can I learn?
2. **Gift of practice**: What can I practice?
3. **Gift of intention**: What is this prompting me to do?

If you are teaching a lesson and it doesn't go well,

1. You could say, "Well, I just learned something that didn't work," or maybe you learned something about yourself or your students. These would be examples of the gift of learning.
2. Or you could say, "I just got a chance to practice, and now I think next time I'll do better." When something doesn't turn out the way you anticipated, you could ask yourself, "What did I practice?" This shifts your attention from dwelling on the gap between what you wanted to happen and the actual results to how the process of what you did helped make you more capable or stronger.
3. You might say, "Now I'm going to . . ." The third type of gift is choosing to do something. You might pull together a few teachers to discuss the situation to come up with alternatives. You could decide to reward yourself with doing one of your hobbies or reaching out to someone you haven't talked to in a while as a gift to yourself for trying.

In that third example, note that there are two different types of gifts of intention. Pulling together a few teachers to discuss the situation is doing something directly related to the outcome. In that example, what you decide to do is directly related to improving the situation caused by the problem. Spending time on a hobby or some other reward is doing something unrelated to the outcome but pleasurable. You might say, "That didn't work out, but I tried, and I'm going to reward myself for trying by going for a pedicure after work."

Here is a personal example. I love to buy wine, but my wife has said that we have too much wine so I should not buy any more for quite a while. And she's probably right, as always, but I really love to buy wine.

Where this comes into play is that sometimes she will do things that really piss me off. Like I'll put an important piece of paper on the dining room table, and she'll throw it out, and I won't find out for a day or so until I really need it. She'll just matter-of-factly say, "If you wanted it, you shouldn't have left it on the table." And as you can guess, that used to make me really angry, and we'd go downhill from there.

Or, you know, she might do any of the things one spouse does that annoys the other one—we all have them and we all do it.

Well, I used to get really upset when that happened, but now, when it happens, I just say to myself, Okay, she's just given you permission to buy another bottle of wine. I don't get angry for long, I don't dwell on it, and I get to do something I love. We don't get into a fight. I'm no longer angry. I'm happy. Problem solved.

Being in the Sage mindset is about how you feel, not what you do. If I were buying wine out of anger or to get even with my wife, then buying the wine would be a limbic, not a Sage action. If I were to buy wine, and my wife were to get angry with me, and then I persisted to buy wine again, I still wouldn't be acting from Sage. I buy the wine as a reward for myself for not going into survivor brain, and my wife understands and accepts that. We actually have a pretty strong partnership.

This example shows that instead of focusing on our anger, fear, or anxiety, we can use some negative result as an excuse to do something that will make us very happy. Think of something that you really love that you don't normally do for yourself. Probably not something expensive, just something that you wouldn't ordinarily allow yourself to do or have. The goal is to celebrate your effort and resilience, not to dwell on the setback but to help you recharge.

All of these examples have been about using the Sage perspective *after* things did not work out as well as one expected. Our limbic brains often freeze us from acting by *imagining* some catastrophe because whatever we do might blow up, just like Casey catastrophizing about not doing well on a test.

Looking at something that already happened, we did something and it didn't work out. We can look for what we learned, we can look for what it gave us a chance to practice, or we can use that to inspire us to take action in some way.

Looking ahead, we face times when we are anxious about doing something. There's some fear that it's not going to work out, which our limbic system interprets as danger, and then our Part X floods us with reasons to fight, flee, or maybe freeze.

Using the Sage perspective or radical acceptance, when we are anxious about something that hasn't happened yet, we can look ahead and accept or convert. We can accept that whatever happens, it is really not that important, so we will be able to live with it, and so there is no reason to be anxious. Or we can decide to convert the outcome to a gift or opportunity, that whether or not we achieve what we want, we can choose what we are going to learn. Or, whether or not we achieve what we want, just the practice is going to increase our abilities. Or we can say, If this doesn't work, I'm going to do X, which is the silver lining.

As David Goggins says in *Never Finished: Unshackle Your Mind and Win the War Within*,

> It's an unwritten natural law of the universe that you will be tested. It will always be up to you to find the lesson in every shitty situation and use it to become stronger, wiser, and better. The best life lessons don't appear when things go well. It's when all your goals and pretty plans turn to shit that you can see your flaws and learn more about yourself. Cultivating a willingness to succeed despite any and all circumstances is the most important variable of the reengagement equation. Your willingness to succeed builds self-esteem. It broadens your concept of your own capability, yet it is the first thing we lose touch with when things go bad.[1]

The Sage perspective is what enables the willingness to succeed despite any and all circumstances. The Sage perspective is about either *converting* any results into a gift or opportunity or *accepting* that any negative results just won't matter. Accept or convert. Those are our two options of the Sage perspective.

---

[1] These are all from the book *Never Finished*, but they occurred in different parts of the book. I took some liberty to assemble them into one paragraph.

The Sage Perspective Summary

- Accept: will these negative results really matter in 5 or 10 years?
- Convert to a gift:
    - What can I learn?
    - What can I practice?
    - What can I do?
        - What can I do to make this situation better?
        - What can I do to make myself feel better?

The Sage brain is very powerful, and as Dr. Stutz points out in the Netflix documentary, our highest moments of joy are when we are overcoming obstacles and our own Part X so that we are able to do and get what we want. As Stutz says in the documentary, "The secret of life is realizing you won't figure it out ever. Nobody else will figure it out. Happiness depends on how you accept that and what you do about it."

Strengths into Saboteurs

No Sage victory is ever permanent. Our Saboteurs and Part X are very wily. One of the weapons the survival brain uses is to turn our strengths into Saboteurs.

Let's say that empathy is a particular strength of ours. We enjoy connecting with people. We are good at finding out what they want and then devising ways to help them. It makes us feel good to see other people happy. That's Sage.

Part X or the Judge twists that power to make it fear-based instead of joy-based. The Judge tells us that if we don't do what people say or what people want that they won't like us or respect us. We start feeling that we *have* to do whatever others want. This is what Shirzad Chamine calls the hyper-pleaser Saboteur, and it's based on fear.

With the hyper-pleaser, you take a lens of always trying to please other people, and a fear that if you do or say or don't do or say certain things, they won't like you or respect you. You may manifest this in not talking candidly to people in order to avoid conflict, in which case you are merely avoiding conflict instead of working to resolve it. Or you may feel that you need to defer to others because if you don't they won't like you. These hyper-pleaser feelings actually sabotage your efforts to grow and achieve. Empathy is the power, but codependency and over-pleasing can be

Saboteurs. And there are similar Saboteurs for each of the Sage powers, summarized in the table below.

Resourcefulness Turned Saboteur

Strength	Saboteur Fear	Saboteur
Empathy	Fear that people won't like us	Hyper-pleaser
Exploration	Fear that we always need more info before acting Fear of missing out	Avoider Restless
Innovation	Fear that no one else can do this Fear that only my ideas will work Fear that it has to be perfect	Hyper-achiever
Navigation	Fear that it's not going to make a difference Fear that no one can analyze this but me Fear that nothing ever goes right for me	Restless Hyper-rational Victim
Focused action	Fear that I have to control everything, or it won't work Fear that I have to account for everything that could possibly go wrong	Hyper-controller Hyper-vigilant

All Saboteurs are based on fear.

If you are good at exploration, you are good at gathering information and not locking into a solution too early. The Judge may twist that into the **restless Saboteur** so you move from thing to thing without completing any, based possibly on fear of missing out. Or it may twist that to the **avoider Saboteur** so that you are always trying to get more information and never moving into action because you are afraid that something bad is going to happen unless you determine the perfect solution beforehand.

If you are good at innovation, you are probably good at pulling together ideas from different sources and analyzing and synthesizing them to come up with novel solutions to solve problems. The Judge can twist that with the fear that no one else can come up with a solution as good as yours or that only you can do something well. That **hyper-achiever Saboteur**, based on the fear that no one else can do it, has thus turned your ability to innovate into a Saboteur trait by your limbic mind.

You may be great at thinking big picture; you know what is most important and can direct the proper effort and resources to achieving what is going to make the biggest difference. This means navigation is one of your strengths. But your Judge can twist that so that you rationalize dropping projects early because they were not really that important or worth the effort (**restless Saboteur**), or that no one else can come up with solutions so you have to control the problem-solving process (**hyper-rational Saboteur**). Or it can twist that to convince you that bad things always happen to you, and you can't ever reach what you want, so you might as well give up (**victim Saboteur**).

And then, you might excel in making things happen. You are good at anticipating or overcoming obstacles, meeting objections, getting projects done well and on time. Your Judge can twist that same planning ability to insist that you have to micromanage and criticize everyone when they don't measure up (**hyper-controller Saboteur**), or it can make you so fearful about what might go wrong that you don't end up taking action (**hyper-vigilant Saboteur**).

We all probably recognize these Saboteurs in ourselves. We all have them. The trick is to recognize them before or just after they manifest themselves. To combat these Saboteurs, we need to recognize them when they occur (using the Interrupter) and then calm our limbic brains to be able to tap into our Sage brains. That should sound familiar.

Saboteur Recognition Hints

We can recognize when our hyper-pleaser Saboteur has put us in survival brain when

- We feel that expressing our own needs is selfish
- We are worried that insisting on our own needs will drive others away
- We are resentful about being taken for granted
- We are anxious that people don't or won't like us

We can recognize our avoider Saboteur when we feel that

- An action is unpleasant, and that maybe if we let it go, it will take care of itself
- If we deal with something now, we will hurt someone's feelings, so we'd rather not
- If we have a conflict with someone, we will lose our connection with them
- Messing with a situation will create a scene

We can recognize our restless Saboteur when

- We are feeling impatience with what is happening now
- We start obsessing over what is next
- We experience fear of missing out

- We are afraid that by staying the course, our unpleasant feelings will grow and become overwhelming
- We are feeling restless and that the others who want to keep going are idiots

We can recognize our hyper-achiever Saboteur when

- We feel we have to be the best at what we do
- We feel that if we can't be exceptional we won't bother
- We know we have to be efficient and effective or something really bad will happen
- All we are thinking about is how successful we have to be, and that if we are not, then we are unworthy

We can recognize our hyper-rational Saboteur when

- We feel we are fully rational and that feelings, and especially others' feelings, are distracting and irrelevant
- We believe other people are sloppy and irrational with their thinking
- We need to shut out any new information or objections as intrusions
- We feel that our self-worth is based on us mastering knowledge and competence

We can recognize our victim Saboteur when

- We think no one understands us
- We are thinking "Poor me"
- We feel that terrible things always happen to us
- We are feeling alone, lonely, and abandoned
- We feel envy and are making negative comparisons of ourselves to others

We can recognize our hyper-controller Saboteur when

- We are feeling that if we are not fully in control, we are out of control
- We have high anxiety when things are not going our way
- We are angry and intimidating because others are not following us
- We feel we are doing others a favor by telling them what to do
- We believe that if we work hard enough, we will be able to control the situation

We can recognize our hyper-vigilant Saboteur when

- We are waiting for the other shoe to drop
- We are afraid that if we make a mistake, everyone is going to jump down our throats

- We acknowledge we would like to trust people, but simultaneously we are suspicious of their motives
- We are anxious or stressed and feel we have to do something immediately
- We believe that life is full of dangers, and that things will fall apart unless we micromanage the situation
- We are reducing a situation to two choices, one bad and the other not quite as bad

We've covered that we can't out-argue our Saboteurs. If we are hyper-pleasing or acting in a way to please people because we are afraid they won't like or respect us, we can't use logic or facts to tap into our Sage brain.

Generally, when we are in Saboteur or limbic mode, we are feeling or thinking a combination of these indicators. We have covered many self-talk techniques, and many of those are multifunctional; they often work in any limbic mode situation. For any of the Saboteurs, just calling it out can sometimes be enough:

- This is just my _____ Saboteur lying to me.
- Hey, _____ Saboteur, stop messing with me.
- _____ Saboteur, thank you for your concern; I'm good now.

Here are a few that apply to specific Saboteurs:

Saboteur	Positive self-talk
Hyper-pleaser	What would be good for both of us, and where should I place boundaries?
	I know people like me and that my hyper-pleaser is sabotaging me; how can I communicate my needs in a way that is assertive yet respectful of others?
Avoider	What is something I can do right now?
	If I start this, and if things don't go right, what will the gift be?
	How will I feel after completing this? What exactly will that be like?
Restless	How can I focus on the present moment and trust the process?
	What different perspectives might be helpful even if I start off by disagreeing?
Hyper-achiever	How can I learn and grow from this experience because of any possible setbacks?
	What do I enjoy about this, regardless of the outcome?

Saboteur	Positive self-talk
Hyper-rational	What can I learn from others' perspectives, even if they seem irrational to me? In what ways does my self-worth go beyond my intellectual achievements?
Victim	What are five things I am grateful for? What strengths and qualities do I possess that I admire in others?
Hyper-controller	What are the potential benefits of allowing others to take the lead or contribute their ideas? How can I balance hard work with the acceptance that some outcomes are beyond my control?
Hyper-vigilant	What evidence is there that things might go well? What would it look like to give someone the benefit of the doubt, and why might that work?

The statements and questions above are just examples. Once you are in Sage mode, once your limbic mind is quieted, your Sage mind will naturally use its empathy, explore, innovate, navigate, and focused action powers to help you move forward.

One more form of self-talk that often works is to call on one of the Sage powers or the Sage perspective:

- How can I use empathy for myself and others here?
- What information would I like to explore?
- How can we use dreamer, realist, critic here to innovate?
- What do I most want from this situation? What would my wiser elder self say to me?
- When I start this and my Saboteurs start trying to make me anxious about continuing, how will I recognize them and quiet them?

Those are a lot of examples of Saboteurs to be aware of and counteract.

I'd like to offer a suggestion.

Take a moment and think of some challenge you are facing or will face soon.

As you think about that challenge, go through the Saboteur recognition hints from a few pages ago and jot down which Saboteurs are likely to have a party in your head.

Once you have the list of Saboteurs, try out some of the possible self-talk suggestions from the table above and write down the answers.

Now, choose one of the five Sage powers: empathy, exploration, innovation, navigation, or focused action. Ask yourself, "If I were to embody that power, how would I act in this situation when these Saboteurs try to kidnap me?"

Now how do you feel about that challenge?

Congratulations! You've just inoculated yourself with a dose of MindShifting.

Chapter 6 Review

Let's return to Maureen.

She and her husband had discovered a leak in their bathroom, and her Saboteurs were having a party in her head: fear, anxiety, and victimhood were dictating freeze, flight, and fight responses.

Maureen recognized the Saboteur lies:

- Victim: why do things always happen to me?
- Hyper-achiever: I need to be an expert or I'm worthless.
- Hyper-pleaser: if I can't figure out and do what my husband wants, he won't respect me.
- Hyper-controller: I need to fix this since my husband hasn't done anything about this.
- Hyper-vigilant: this is just the beginning. Fixing this and all the other problems is going to take a lot of time and money that we don't have.

Maureen first used positive self-talk to halt her journey into deeper and deeper limbic mode. She called out the Saboteurs with "These are all just my Saboteurs scaring me—it's a story. In fact, it's just a small leak, nothing structural seems to have broken, and we've fixed problems before."

She took some time to focus on her breathing while she and her husband made some small talk and jokes about the situation that eased the tension.

They then explored where the leak was, what likely caused it, and looked up potential ways to fix it. As they were doing this, she shared with her husband how she was using her Interrupter and Self-Commander to stay in resilient mode, and that seemed to calm him as well. They decided that they would work together to fix the pipe themselves, made a plan of action, reached out to a friend who was a plumber to check that it was reasonable, and slowly started working on the leak over the next day. She remarked, "It was weird but amazing how this stressful situation was handled with awareness, and there were no overwhelming feelings. I didn't feel fearless, but the feelings felt manageable. And now I feel ready for more projects with my husband."

What Maureen did was the essence of self-regulation. As Stuart Shanker notes in *Self-Reg: How to Help Your Child (and You) Break the Stress Cycle and Successfully Engage with Life*, self-regulation is about identifying the causes and reducing the intensity of impulses, and, when necessary, having the energy to resist.

Or, as Dr. Becky Kennedy says in *Good Inside: A Guide to Becoming the Parent You Want to Be*, avoiding fear and distress is not the same as moving toward happiness. Resilience is happiness. Resilience is the ability to experience a wide range of emotions and still feel like ourselves. People who are resilient are better able to cope when stressful moments arise. Resilience occurs when we don't know that we will succeed, when we can handle the doubts and not let them become anxiety or fear. Resilience and happiness occur when we can tolerate and work through stress instead of avoid and make a beeline out of stress.

Just like Maureen did, and, hopefully, like the tools of this book have shown you to do.

The End?

These chapters have focused on concepts and tools to give you control over your mind.

Our minds are not designed to determine the truth, but for actions that lead to survival. Our brains perceive what is helpful, not what is true. By default, we accept those thoughts as reality, but they are just stories.

In this book, you've learned techniques to recognize when you are in a story or following a script, methods of quieting the internal critical voices, and then how to tap into your creativity, critical thinking, and resourcefulness.

When we accept the feelings, stories, and ideas that get generated by our limbic minds, we react. When we learn to take a step back, question, generate alternatives, and proceed with ease and flow, we respond.

Theoretically, if you were able to apply these techniques each time you were stuck in limbic mode, you'd never be stuck reacting for long.

It sounds easier than it is.

Practically, there will always be times when your Part X and Saboteurs trigger you. There will be situations where you struggle to find ways of moving forward. There will be people who oppose your best plans or even try to sabotage you.

And those struggles, as tough and exasperating as they are while you are going through them, are going to be your biggest triumphs.

Hopefully you've been able to apply these already and have noticed an increase in your own effectiveness and joy in living.

Please use whichever of these techniques help you lead a richer, happier life. The material in this book is primarily taken from the course MindShifting: Mastering Your Resilient Mind.

In addition to that course, I also teach two other courses, Flexible Mindsets for Long-Term Success, and Conflict and Collaboration. Those courses are all run through the MindShifting Educators Community.

It really helps when you can go into events knowing what is likely to trigger you and how to steel your mind to prepare for unexpected results. That's the basis of the second MindShifting course, MindShifting: Flexible Mindsets for Long-Term Success, and that will be the title of the second book, if there is one.

It also helps if you are pre-armed for how to respond when people get in the way. The third course, MindShifting: Conflict and Collaboration, is all about working with others. If there is a third book, that will be the subject.

If enough people read this book, I can write additional books based on the other two courses.

Let's see if we can make a difference in the lives of five million people.

Acknowledgments

If you have enjoyed reading this book, please take some time to appreciate the contributions of all of us who helped make this book a reality. I may be listed as the author of this book, but I was just one person of the many who made this book possible.

Of course, there were all the sources that are listed in Author's Resources. Almost none of the ideas in this book originated with me. All I've done is curate concepts and techniques from a wide variety of fields. The authors listed in the sources are the true innovators who devised and then tested these methods.

Robbi Nierenberg at https://www.coachrobbi.com/ was my Positive Intelligence coach for three years. She mentored me and a host of others on the nuances of the Sage Powers, Saboteurs, and the Sage Perspective and how to apply them to our lives and teaching.

My wife is my number one teacher, and she also suggested the Preface. You quickly discover the importance of MindShifting when you go on a "short flat" bicycle ride with her.

Kader Kaneye is the founder of African Development University in Niamey, Niger. ADU's mission is to prepare the next generation to lead Africa. He was the person who first asked me to teach Sensemaking to university students, which inspired the development of the first MindShifting course and led, seven years later, to this book. So many ADU students have gone on to lead remarkable lives!

Tammie Schrader participated in the first online class of MindShifting and has continued to encourage educators to learn MindShifting techniques. Tammie is a world-respected proponent of STEM, STEAM, game-based learning, and the use of technology to inspire children to learn and excel.

Nancy Mangum, Kristin Ziemke, Theresa Gibbons, and Darren Hudgins have refined many MindShifting techniques for educators and have been a wonderful source of ideas and feedback on what works. They all coach educators and educational leaders in techniques to ignite student passion, creativity, and critical thinking.

Laura Zug at https://www.laurazug.com/ ordered me to produce a book instead of just the three MindShifting courses. Laura helps people with life missions through classes and her Hive community to build communities to improve the world.

Elizabeth Thorlton patiently and professionally edited this book, with hundreds of suggestions to improve its readability.

Kimb Manson Williams captured the essence of MindShifting with the book cover graphic, which shows a brain with an active limbic system no longer shackled to an individual who is moving toward a prefrontal cortex activated brain.

Judy Weintraub orchestrated the book publishing. She runs SkillBites, https://skillbites.net/, which guides subject matter experts through all the intricacies of producing and publishing high-quality books.

Together, we built this book and hopefully more to come.

Author's Resources

1. American Psychological Association, *Mindfulness Resources* https://bit.ly/3AMsKrk
2. Aguilar, Elena, *Onward: Cultivating Emotional Resilience in Educators*
3. Ariely, Dan, *Predictably Irrational*
4. Blanchard, Ken, Zigarmi, Patricia, and Zigarmi, Drea, *Leadership and the One Minute Manager Updated Edition: Increasing Effectiveness Through Situational Leadership II*
5. Blanchett, Michelle, and Deters, Brian, *Preventing Polarization: 50 Strategies for Teaching Kids About Empathy, Politics, and Civic Responsibility*
6. Botsman, Rachel, "Why Anticipation is a Powerful Creative Space," https://bit.ly/4enxdP2
7. Brown, Adrienne Maree, *Emergent Strategy: Shaping Change, Changing Worlds*
8. Brown, Adrienne Maree, *Holding Change: The Way of Emergent Strategy Facilitation and Mediation*
9. Chamine, Shirzad, *Positive Intelligence: Why Only 20% of Teams and Individuals Achieve Their True Potential AND HOW YOU CAN ACHIEVE YOURS*
10. Csikszentmihalyi, Mihaly, *Creativity: The Psychology of Discovery and Invention*
11. Csikszentmihalyi, Mihaly, *The Evolving Self: A Psychology for the Third Millennium*
12. Dávila, Ximena, and Maturana, Humberto, *La revolución reflexiva*
13. Dilts, Robert Brian, Epstein, Todd, and Dilts, Robert Warren, *Tools for Dreamers: Strategies for Creativity and the Structure of Innovation*

14. Doty, James R., MD, *Into the Magic Shop: A Neurosurgeon's Quest to Discover the Mysteries of the Brain and the Secrets of the Heart*
15. Fischer, Joern, and Reichers, Maraja, "A leverage points perspective on sustainability," https://bit.ly/3YIPL6B
16. Goggins, David, *Can't Hurt Me: Master Your Mind and Defy the Odds*
17. Goggins, David, *Never Finished: Unshackle Your Mind and Win the War Within*
18. Grant, Adam, *Think Again: The Power of Knowing What You Don't Know*
19. Harari, Yuval Noah, *21 Lessons for the 21st Century*
20. Harari, Yuval Noah, *Homo Deus: A Brief History of Tomorrow*
21. Harari, Yuval Noah, *Sapiens: A Brief History of Humankind*
22. Harris, Nadine Burke, MD, *The Deepest Well: Healing the Long-Term Effects of Childhood Adversity*
23. Herman, Judith Lewis, MD, *Truth and Repair: How Trauma Survivors Envision Justice*
24. Hill, Jonah, *Stutz* (Netflix documentary about psychiatrist/therapist Phil Stutz)
25. Ichioka, Sarah, and Pawlyn, Michael, *Flourish: Design Paradigms for Our Planetary Emergency*
26. Jeevan, Sharath, *Intrinsic: A manifesto to reignite your inner drive*
27. Jetter, Rick, *100 No-Nonsense things that ALL TEACHERS Should Stop Doing*
28. Johnson, Steven, *Farsighted: How We Make the Decisions That Matter the Most*
29. Kurtz, CF, and Snowden, DJ, "The new dynamics of strategy: Sense-making in a complex and complicated world"
30. List, Friedrich, The National System of Political Economy, https://bit.ly/3YzZNGY (translated from German by Sampson S. Lloyd)
31. Llinás, Rodolfo R., *I of the Vortex: From Neurons to Self*
32. London, Laura, Madner, Stephanie, and Skerritt, Dominic, "How many people are really needed in a transformation?" https://mck.co/3ApB0O7
33. Luo, Yangmei, et al., "Well-being and Anticipation for Future Positive Events: Evidences from an fMRI Study," https://bit.ly/3YWnbA2
34. McGonigal, Jane, *Imaginable: How to See the Future Coming and Feel Ready for Anything, Even Things That Seem Impossible Today*
35. Meadows, Donella, "Leverage Points: Places to Intervene in a System," https://bit.ly/3Cj1tgB

36. National Institutes of Health, "Meditation and Mindfulness: Effectiveness and Safety," https://bit.ly/3CeSZHl

37. Ranganath, Charan, *Why We Remember: Unlocking Memory's Power to Hold on to What Matters*

38. Ripley, Amanda, *High Conflict: Why We Get Trapped and How We Get Out*

39. Rose, Todd, *Collective Illusions: Conformity, Complicity, and the Science of Why We Make Bad Decisions*

40. Rose, Todd, *The End of Average: How We Succeed in a World That Values Sameness*

41. Rosenberg, Alex, *How History Gets Things Wrong: The Neuroscience of Our Addiction to Stories*

42. Rosenberg, Marshall B. and Chopra, Deepak, *Nonviolent Communication: A Language of Life*

43. Sachs, Jonah, *Unsafe Thinking: How to be Nimble and Bold When You Need It Most*

44. Satell, Greg, "To Implement Change, You Don't Need to Convince Everyone at Once," https://bit.ly/3CeT4e7

45. Shanker, Stuart, *Self-Reg: How to Help Your Child (and You) Break the Stress Cycle and Successfully Engage with Life*

46. Smil, Vaclav, *How the World Really Works: The Science Behind How We Got Here and Where We're Going*

47. Snowden, DJ, *The Cynefin Co*, https://thecynefin.co/our-thinking/

48. Taleb, Nassim Nicholas, *Antifragile: Things That Gain from Disorder*

49. Taleb, Nassim Nicholas, *Fooled by Randomness: The Hidden Role of Chance in Life and in the Markets*

50. Taylor-Lopez, Louise, *Activation Exercise*, https://smartpa.ge/KimH

51. Thompson, Helen, *Disorder: Hard Times in the 21st Century*

52. Walther, Cornelia C., *Technology, Social Change and Human Behavior: Influence for Impact*

53. Warshay, Danny, *See, Solve, Scale: How Anyone Can Turn an Unsolved Problem into a Breakthrough Success*

54. Willingham, Daniel T., *Why Don't Students Like School?: A Cognitive Scientist Answers Questions About How the Mind Works and What It Means for the Classroom*

55. Wolf, Mary Ann, *Leading Personalized and Digital Learning: A Framework for Implementing School Change*

www.ingramcontent.com/pod-product-compliance
Lightning Source LLC
Chambersburg PA
CBHW081446070526
44586CB00019B/2249